Nebraska Kitchens
COOKBOOK
VOLUME 2
Favorite Recipes of Our State

Recipes from the readers of *Nebraska Life Magazine.*

NEBRASKA
LIFE

Published by
Nebraska Life Publishing, Inc.
Norfolk, Nebraska
1-800-777-6159
www.NebraskaLife.com

Cover photo: Fudge Puddles. See pg. 89 for recipe.

Nebraska Kitchens

FAVORITE RECIPES OF OUR STATE

GUM DROP BARS, PG. 88

THE BEST SUNDAY DINNER

THE "NEBRASKA KITCHENS" CONCEPT started with a Sunday dinner at grandmother's house.

Because she doesn't cook anymore it was our turn to treat – a bucket of chicken and two sides of slaw, which got us talking about those good meals we used to have when grandma cooked.

My favorite was the Wednesday evening tradition of crock pot roast beef with mashed potatoes. Her favorite was fruit soup, a dish I remembered for the sweet, moist smell it left in the air of her house. Stewed raisins, apples and plums simmering with sour cream and dumplings sent us grandkids home with full bellies and fond memories.

But *her* memories are what she sent home with us that Sunday afternoon. Memories and stories of our pioneering, sod-busting Wayne County farm family. In particular, she told a story of when she was a 16-year-old girl. Her father became ill with lung cancer and sought radium treatments in Rochester.

Her mother became manager of the farm, farmhands and horses. They moved his bed to the living room and hired a nurse to care for him during the day.

Above, diners enjoy "crab boil" at the Feed Barn restaurant in Mitchell. Opposite, the Hoff family at the coffeehouse inside Alliance's Hoffhaus Gardens and pages from the "Nebraska Kitchens" section of *Nebraska Life Magazine.*

from the Recipe File of Maggie and Alta

Refrigerator Pickles

2 cups Sugar
2 cups Vinegar
1/4 cup salt (scant)
1 1/2 tsp tumeric (1 1/3)
mustard seed.

He would awake at night with hunger for just one food: fruit soup. Her mother obliged and filled their house with the sweet, moist smelling, late-night meals for a failing farmer.

Toward the end, an owl perched above the portico columns outside their living room window and hoot, hoot, hooted my grandmother awake. Her father passed in the spring, and the owl never returned. The Great Depression started the next year.

This was an important time in my grandmother's life, and her story was relayed to us first-hand because of a simple meal and the shared memories of food. It was the best Sunday dinner.

It inspired us to begin asking the readers of *Nebraska Life Magazine* (nearly 100,000 of them) for their recipes and stories – stories of food, family and life in Nebraska. The popular "Nebraska Kitchens" section was born! Then came the original *Nebraska Kitchens Cookbook* and finally this new *Nebraska Kitchens Cookbook, Volume 2.*

One cook whose story appears in this book summed up the Nebraska Kitchens concept: "These are more than recipes; these are memories of people who have shaped my life."

Heirloom and modern, healthy and hearty, these are Nebraska's recipes and stories. We hope you'll enjoy reading them and that they'll inspire you to find your "best" Sunday dinner.

- Christopher Amundson
Publisher and Editor
Nebraska Life Magazine

NEBRASKA KITCHENS

NEBRASKA KITCHENS has proved so popular with readers that we've decided to put together a *Nebraska Life* cookbook. That means we'll need even more of your favorite recipes. We're especially interested in recipes that have been passed from one generation to the next – main courses, soups, breads, desserts, veggie dishes and salads, ethnic and seasonal dishes. (See p. 81 for details.) Some, like the ones presented here, will be selected for Nebraska Kitchens as well!

Recipes prepared by Danette Bristow

Tomato-Pepper Relish

Janice Gordon of North, Va., sends a recipe from her great-grandmother, Carrie Fallon, who came to Nebraska in 1879. According to Janice's mother's notes on the recipe, "Salads as we know them were quite unheard of in Grandmother's day. This recipe filled the bill quite well in the pioneer menu. Grandma came from England at the age of 15, was married to Pat Fallon, and their first home was a dugout north of Elkhorn. Near this site the family farm home was later established and was well known for many years in Douglas County, as was Grandma Fallon for her culinary skill."

8 firm garden-ripe tomatoes
2 large green peppers
2 medium-size onions
1 tablespoon coarse salt

Chop vegetables and toss together with salt. Let stand for a few minutes or longer before serving. Excellent with fried chicken and roasting ears.

Warm Pineapple Salad

"This recipe came from my mother, Sue Gueck Ehrman," writes Joan Koehler of Scottsbluff. "She was one of those cooks who could whip up a traditional meat and potatoes meal for a crew of farm hands, but also had an eye for the unusual new recipe. This is one of her salads, a little different, but just wait till you try it! Somebody always makes it for our family get-togethers."

1 large can (16-20 oz) crushed pineapple
1 egg, beaten
1/2 cup sugar
2 Tbsp cornstarch
1 cup mini marshmallows
3/4 cup shredded sharp cheddar cheese

Combine egg, sugar, cornstarch and pineapple in pan. Heat and cook until thickened. Add cheese and mix well. Pour into an 8 x 8 or 9 x 9 pan and top with mini marshmallows. Bake at 300° for 10 minutes or until brown on top.

Best Cinnamon Rolls

Elizabeth Drake of B...

TRIPLE BERRY ZUCCHINI BREAD, PG. 8

APPLE STICKY BUNS, PG. 12

PECAN PIE MUFFINS, PG. 19

BLUEBERRY ORANGE BAKED PANCAKE, PG. 11

Breads & Rolls

When unexpected company would come on Sunday afternoon, my mother would mix up a batch of donuts, place them on a step stool over the furnace vent in the kitchen to rise and fry fresh donuts for afternoon lunch before the company went home. Needless to say, we seldom needed anything more for supper.

– Mary Heusman

2 large eggs, lightly beaten
2 ¼ cups raw sugar
1 cup canola oil
3 tsp vanilla
2 cups grated zucchini
3 cups unbleached, organic all-purpose flour
1 Tbsp baking powder
1/4 tsp baking soda
1 tsp salt
1 tsp cinnamon
2 cups fresh or frozen berries

Makes 3 loaves
or 5-6 mini loaves

Triple Berry Zucchini Bread
Osmond

Every spring, Nebraskans face an important decision – whether to plant their own zucchini, or to just wait for the neighbors to show up. Either way, you're getting some. And no matter whether you grow it or get it, you'll probably have an abundance. Melissa Lind sent in this unique zucchini recipe. It's one of her favorite ways to use all that zucchini.

"I modified this recipe to use more natural and organic ingredients and all the zucchini that shows up on my door step," she writes. "I bring it to work all the time and give it away as food gifts to friends and neighbors."

Preheat oven to 350°. Grease 5 or 6 mini loaf pans, or 3 bread size loaf pans.

In large mixing bowl beat eggs, sugar, oil and vanilla. Add zucchini and mix well. In separate bowl combine flour with baking powder, soda, salt and cinnamon. Beat in flour mixture, one cup at a time. Fold in berries. Fill pans two-thirds full. Bake 1 hour or until toothpick comes out clean.

Evan's Crescent Rolls

Norfolk

"Evan has been cooking with me since he was two," writes his grandmother, Linda Unkel of Norfolk. "Evan is very involved in 4-H and won first place at the Madison County Fair for his crescent rolls. Evan (now 11) makes up his own recipes and his own designs in woodworking, also winning prizes. We are very proud of Evan."

1	package active dry yeast
1/4	cup warm water
1	cup milk, scalded
1/4	cup sugar
1/4	cup shortening
1	tsp salt
3 ½	cups sifted all-purpose flour
1	egg

MAKES 12 ROLLS

Soften yeast in warm water (110°). Combine milk, sugar, shortening and salt; cool to lukewarm. Add 1½ cups of flour; beat well. Beat in yeast and egg. Gradually add remaining flour to form soft dough, beating well. Place in greased bowl, turning once to grease surface. Cover and let rise until doubled (1 ½-2 hours).

Turn out on lightly floured surface and shape as desired. Cover and let shaped rolls rise until doubled (30-45 minutes). Bake on greased baking sheet or in greased muffin pans at 400° for 12-15 minutes.

Etta's Donuts

Lakeside

1 cup sugar
3 Tbsp melted butter
2 tsp baking powder
1 tsp salt
3/4 cup milk
3 cups flour
1 tsp mace or nutmeg
2 egg yolks
(save egg whites)

MAKES 24 DONUTS

"My mother, Etta Hamilton, fed the army of men who dug us out of the blizzard of '49 on these donuts," writes Gail Glassgow of Lakeside. "We had been snowed in for days, and mom made this big batch of donuts when we heard the sound of dozers and other big equipment clearing the roads. My dad said, 'The Lord brought us the men and you brought them donuts!' "

Beat egg whites stiff. Mix all ingredients except egg whites together well. Gently fold in egg whites last. Roll on floured board to 1/4-inch thick. Cut with donut cutter. Fry in oil or lard at 385°, turning often. Drain on paper towel; may roll in granulated sugar.

Yeast Donuts

Eddyville

2 cake yeast cubes or
  2 packages dry yeast
5 cups lukewarm milk
2 tsp salt
2 eggs
6 Tbsp sugar
3 Tbsp melted
  shortening or butter
8-10 cups flour

GLAZE
1 tsp vanilla
1 lb powered sugar
  Milk as needed by
  ½ teaspoonfuls

MAKES 5-6 DOZEN

"This recipe was handed down to me from my mother," writes Mary Heusman of Eddyville. "When unexpected company would come on Sunday afternoon, she would mix up a batch of donuts, place them on a step stool over the furnace vent in the kitchen to rise, and fry fresh donuts for afternoon lunch before the company went home. Needless to say, we seldom needed anything more for supper."

In large mixing bowl, let yeast, milk, sugar, salt, shortening and eggs set until yeast gets soft, then add 2 cups flour and beat well. Add flour gradually until dough can be handled. Turn out on floured board and knead. Let rise until doubled. Turn out on lightly floured board and pat out to about 1/2-inch thick. Cut out donuts and let rise about 20 minutes. Fry in oil at 375°, turning to brown evenly.

Combine vanilla, powdered sugar and milk to make a soft frosting. Dip donuts in a shallow pan of frosting while they are hot.

BLUEBERRY ORANGE BAKED PANCAKE

Nebraska City

"I usually serve this with an orange and blueberry fruit mixture, served in the orange shell. This is a dish that will impress any guest," writes Jeanna Stavas of Nebraska City. "I found this recipe when staying at a bed and breakfast."

Preheat oven to 350°. Spray a 9 x 13-inch baking pan with cooking spray.

Combine butter and sugar in large bowl to make the batter. Add eggs; beat well. Combine flour and baking powder. Mix flour mixture and milk alternately into butter mixture. Pour half of batter into pan.

To make the filling, in medium bowl, beat eggs, melted butter, salt, cottage cheese and pie filling. Spread filling over batter in the pan. Add remaining batter by spoonfuls to spread as evenly as possible. Bake 50-60 minutes or until golden brown. Let sit 5 minutes to set up before adding topping.

To make the topping, in small saucepan, heat blueberry pie filling just to warm. In small bowl, mix sour cream, vanilla and powdered sugar. You may substitute plain or vanilla yogurt for the sour cream to make a lighter sauce.

Cut baked pancake into squares. Serve with blueberry sauce and a dollop of sour cream sauce, or combine blueberry and sour cream sauce as shown in the photo above. Sprinkle with orange zest.

To make the orange bowls: Using a zester tool, score a whole orange from top to bottom, creating stripes of various widths. Save zest strips for garnish. Slice top and bottom of orange off to create a flat bottom so orange bowls can sit on plate. Cut orange in half. With a sharp knife remove orange flesh from skin. Remove sections of orange and combine with other fruits such as blueberries, grapes or raspberries and fill orange bowls with fruit mixture. Garnish with zest strips.

BATTER

- 1/2 cup butter at room temperature
- 1/4 cup sugar
- 3 eggs
- 1 tsp almond flavoring
- 2 cups flour
- 1 ½ tsp baking powder
- 1 ¼ cups milk

FILLING

- 2 eggs
- 3 Tbsp butter, melted
- 3 cups small curd cottage cheese
- 1 Tbsp blueberry pie filling
- 1 tsp salt

TOPPING

- 1 16-oz can blueberry pie filling
- 1 cup sour cream
- 1 tsp vanilla extract
- 2 Tbsp powdered sugar
  Orange zest strips

SERVES 9-12

3 ¼ cups flour
2 packages quick rise
    yeast
1/4 cup sugar
1 tsp salt
3/4 cup milk
1/4 cup water
1/4 cup margarine,
    cubed
1 egg
2 ½ cups chopped apples
    (Granny Smith or
    Yellow Delicious)

TOPPING
1 cup brown sugar
3/4 cup margarine,
    cubed
3/4 cup chopped nuts
1 Tbsp water
1 Tbsp maple syrup
1 tsp cinnamon

SERVES 12-16

APPLE STICKY BUNS

Ravenna

"This is a treat I make and serve to the truck drivers when they come to load our cattle into the summer pasture or when they bring them home in the fall," writes Donna Pritschau of Ravenna. *"I also take these to meetings, and they are very popular."*

In a large bowl combine 1½ cups flour, yeast, sugar and salt. In a saucepan heat milk, water and margarine. Add to dry ingredients and beat until just moistened. Add egg, beat until smooth. Stir in rest of flour and apples. Cover and let rise 30 minutes. Stir down dough.

In saucepan combine topping ingredients. Put in 13 x 9 x 2-inch baking dish, covering bottom evenly. Spoon pieces of dough over the topping. Cover and let rise for 30 minutes.

Bake at 375° for 30-35 minutes or until golden brown. Let stand 6 minutes and invert on platter.

Apricot Zucchini Bread
Lindsay

"I have done hair for over 40 years and with that comes great friendships," writes Judith Weitzel Wilmink of Lindsay. *"We talk a lot and of course food is one of the topics that we like to talk about. This recipe came from one of my ladies that used to live near Albion and has since moved back to Iowa. I have been making it for at least 25 years and have been sharing the recipe with others too. What a great way to use zucchini in a different way and get our vegetables in also. It's very moist and has a little different twist to it. Hope you enjoy it as much as we do."*

3	eggs
1	cup salad oil
1	cup brown sugar
1/2	cup white sugar
1 ½	tsp vanilla
1 ½	tsp cinnamon
1/2	tsp almond flavoring
3	cups flour
2	tsp soda
1	tsp salt
1/2	tsp baking powder
3/4	tsp nutmeg
1	cup currants (raisins)
1	cup chopped nuts (optional)
1	cup apricot pulp (drain can and mash)
2	cups shredded zucchini

MAKES 2 BREAD PANS
OR 4 SMALL FRUIT PANS

Beat eggs. Add oil, sugars and flavorings. Beat well. Add flour, soda, salt, baking powder, cinnamon and nutmeg. Add currents, nuts, apricot pulp and zucchini. Fold in until blended. Bake at 350° for 40-60 minutes.

Lynda's White Bread
Chadron

"Back in the '70s I started making lots of bread. I've tried many different recipes looking for the perfect one. One day I decided to take a little from several recipes that I liked and came up with the recipe for the best and most perfect white bread you'll ever sink your teeth into," writes Lynda Eckdahl of Chadron.

1/2	cup butter
2/3	cup sugar
1	tsp salt
2 ¼	cups hot milk
1	package active dry yeast
1	egg, beaten
7	cups flour

MAKES 2 LOAVES

In small bowl, combine yeast and 1/4 cup warm water and let sand for 5 minutes. In a saucepan, add butter, sugar, salt and milk. Heat until butter melts. Do not boil. Let cool to lukewarm. Add beaten egg to yeast mixture. In large mixing bowl, add 3 cups flour to milk mixture and mix well. Add yeast mixture and beat vigorously.

Add 3 more cups flour, stirring until dough is extremely thick. Turn out on floured board and knead a minute or so. Let dough rest 10 minutes. Add remaining flour, but only if dough is sticky. Resume kneading until smooth and elastic. Put dough in large buttered bowl, cover and let rise until doubled. Punch down, knead for a minute or two and shape into 2 loaves. Put into buttered loaf pans, cover and let rise until doubled. Bake in preheated 375° oven for 40 minutes.

SOUTHERN GAL BISCUITS
Orchard

2 cups all purpose flour, sifted
4 tsp baking powder
1/2 tsp cream of tartar
1/2 tsp salt
2 Tbsp sugar
1/2 cup shortening
1 egg
2/3 cup milk

MAKES 2 DOZEN BISCUITS

"These never fail and are so light!" writes Betty Jean Gunter of Orchard. "I found this recipe years ago and it's all I ever make."

In large mixing bowl, combine flour, baking powder, cream of tartar, salt and sugar. Cut shortening into flour mixture until crumbly using pastry cutter or mixer. Add egg and milk and mix lightly with wooden spoon until dough is blended. On floured board, roll out dough to 1/2-inch thickness and cut circles with a drinking glass. Brush tops with butter. Bake on cookie sheet at 450° for 10-15.

FAVORITE GRIDDLE CAKES
Wayne

1 ¼ cup flour
1/2 tsp salt
1 Tbsp baking powder
1 Tbsp sugar
1 egg, beaten
1 cup milk
2 Tbsp melted shortening or bacon fat

SERVES 6-8

"We didn't have much money growing up, but what we had mom could stretch," writes Connie Kirkpatrick of Wayne. "This was often our supper meal, and we would have a fried egg, but no meat. She would make her own homemade syrup of brown sugar and water to give us something sweet to put on our griddle cakes. My grandmother passed this to her daughter-in-law, and my mom gave it to me. This was one of my first recipes I had when I got married."

In medium mixing bowl combine flour, salt, baking powder, and sugar. Stir to mix well. In a separate small bowl, combine egg, milk and shortening. Mix liquid ingredients into dry ingredients with whisk or mixer on low speed. Batter should be easy to pour. Add a little milk if necessary. Heat a large skillet or griddle to medium temperature (350° if using an electric griddle). Add just enough grease to cover bottom of pan. Spoon batter by half cup-fulls onto griddle. Turn cakes over when bubbles from batter pop and stay open.

STRAWBERRY BREAD

Syracuse

"My son needed to do a demonstration for a speech class in high school," writes Karen Johnston of Syracuse. "He demonstrated making a grilled cheese sandwich and his classmate demonstrated the strawberry bread. He got the recipe from her and we have been making it ever since."

In large mixing bowl, stir together oil, sugar and eggs. Combine flour, baking soda, cinnamon and salt. Stir until smooth. Add thawed strawberries and mix. Pour batter into two greased loaf pans. Bake at 350° for 1 hour or until toothpick comes out clean.

1 ½	cups vegetable oil
2	cups sugar
3	eggs
3	cups flour
1	tsp baking soda
1	tsp cinnamon
3/4	tsp salt
1	16-oz package frozen strawberries, thawed

MAKES 2 LOAVES

3 cups all purpose
  flour
1 ½ cup light brown
  sugar
1 tsp baking soda
3/4 tsp salt
1/2 cup shortening
1/4 cup buttermilk or
  sour milk to moisten

SERVES 12

"A.P." CAKES

Ainsworth

"Grandma Ann Peal would bake these coffee cakes and set them on the window sill to cool, and the cakes would be stolen by the neighborhood kids," writes Bonnie Wolf of Ainsworth. "She started writing her initials in the cakes and friends began calling them A.P. Cakes."

Grease two 8-inch pie pans. Combine all dry ingredients in a large mixing bowl. Add buttermilk to make consistency like soft cookie dough. Divide the dough in two and place in pie pans. Pat with hand or use the back of a spoon to level dough. Bake at 375° for 35-40 minutes.

Christmas Bread

Talmage

"This recipe really came over on the boat from Norway," writes Mary Teten of Talmage.

"Millie Nygard, brought this recipe with her to America, and her daughter, my friend Esther Probst, shared it with me many years ago. Traditionally this is made at Christmas, but Millie, and later Esther, would make loaves and give them away as a gifts of hospitality to welcome new neighbors. I usually make this in rolls, like Parker House or Clover Leaf, rather than loaves."

In small bowl, dissolve yeast in lukewarm water. In very large bowl, pour scalded milk over butter and blend. When milk is cooled to lukewarm, add dissolved yeast and sugar. Add half of the flour and salt and beat well with mixer for 10 minutes. Add eggs one at a time and beat well. Remove mixer and add remaining flour, salt, fruit and cardamom.

Knead and place in a greased bowl and set in warm place to rise. When doubled in size, knead again. Let rise again 30 minutes. Shape into loaves or rolls in greased pans. Beat egg white with fork until foamy. Brush tops of loaves or rolls with beaten egg white. When doubled in size, bake at 350° for 35-40 minutes. Brush crust with melted butter and sprinkle with cinnamon and sugar mixture.

2	package dry yeast
1/2	cup lukewarm water
3	cups milk, scalded
1/2	cup butter
3/4	cup sugar
10	cups bread flour
2	tsp salt
2	eggs
1/2	cup currents
3/4	cup raisins
1/2	cup red and green candied cherries
1/2	tsp cardamom
1	beaten egg white
	Melted butter
	Cinnamon and sugar

MAKES 4 LOAVES
OR 48 ROLLS

Steamed Dumplings

McCook

"This is a favorite recipe from my grandmother," writes Kari Rich of McCook. *"She always had wonderful meals ready for us when we would stop by to visit when I was a child."*

Sift flour, baking powder and salt together. Combine beaten egg, milk and oil. Add to dry ingredients to make soft dough. Drop by spoonfuls into stew or broth. Stew should have 3 cups liquid (add boiling water if necessary). Cover and steam 15 minutes. Serve at once.

1	cup flour
1 ½	tsp baking powder
1/2	tsp salt
1	egg
1/3	cup milk
2	Tbsp melted butter or vegetable oil

MAKES 8 LARGE
DUMPLINGS

1/2 cup sugar
2 packages yeast
2 cups milk
1/2 cup peanut butter
2 tsp salt
4½-5 cups flour

FILLING

1 8-oz package cream
cheese, softened
1/4 cup peanut butter
2 Tbsp flour
1/2 cup powdered sugar

MAKES 2 DOZEN ROLLS

PEANUT BUTTER SWEET ROLLS
Hemingford

"When my daughter played volleyball in high school I made these as a treat for her team several times," writes Sheila King of Hemingford. "These are so tender and tasty, and the girls would make short work of them."

Heat milk until very warm; add sugar and yeast and let rise. Mix in peanut butter and salt. Slowly add flour until you have medium-stiff dough. Cover and let rise until doubled. Divide dough into 2 portions and roll into rectangles. Mix filling ingredients, reserving 1/2 cup. Spread remaining filling evenly on the 2 rectangles. Roll up as for cinnamon rolls. Slice into rolls about 2 inches thick and place into greased baking pans. Let rise until double. Bake at 350° for 25-35 minutes until golden brown. Thin the remaining filling with milk or water to make glaze. Glaze rolls after cooling.

NEVER FAIL ROLLS
Merna

"Our favorite at our family dinners!" writes Shirley Gottula of Merna. "I've given this recipe to all three of my daughters-in-law. We all love the rolls and they are easy to make."

2 packages yeast
2 cups lukewarm water
1/2 cup melted butter
or margarine
1/2 cup sugar
2 tsp salt
3 eggs, beaten
6 ½ cups flour

MAKES 24 ROLLS

Dissolve yeast in water. Beat together butter, eggs, salt and sugar. Stir in yeast water and gradually add flour 2 cups at a time until dough can be handled easily. Knead and place in greased bowl. Turn dough once inside bowl to have top of dough greased. Let rise until doubled. Punch down and shape into rolls. Bake at 400° for 30 minutes.

Pecan Pie Muffins

Edgar

"These muffins are delicious for breakfast with a bowl of fresh fruit," writes Deloris Springer of Edgar. "We often have them as a snack, and I always keep them on hand. I freeze them in small baggies and then they are always fresh."

In a large mixing bowl, combine sugar and butter together, mixing well with a wooden spoon. Add eggs and continue mixing until smooth and creamy. Add flour and nuts. Grease muffin pan or use cupcake liners. Fill each pan section two-thirds full. Bake at 350° for 12-15 minutes.

1	cup light brown sugar
2/3	cup melted butter
2	eggs
1/2	cup all purpose flour
1	cup chopped pecans

Makes 2 dozen muffins or 5 dozen mini-muffins

"Lead" Dumplings

Norfolk

"This recipe was handed down to my mother from her mother-in-law (my grandmother) when she got married. It was used in chicken soup," writes Gayle Frevert of Norfolk. "Chicken dumpling soup is a family tradition and a holiday and winter favorite. 'Lead' is our nickname for them because they are so heavy, compared to baking power dumplings."

In a medium mixing bowl, mix flour and salt. Make a hole in the dry ingredients and add softened shortening. Pour in boiling water on shortening. Let it melt a little and mix. Add eggs one at a time and beat well. Drop dumplings by spoonfuls into hot soup. Simmer for at least 10 minutes. When they float they're done.

12	cups chicken soup or broth
2	cups flour
1	tsp salt
1/2	cup shortening, softened
1/2	cup water, boiling
2	eggs

Serves 6

1 cake yeast
1/2 cup melted butter or shortening
1 tsp granulated sugar
1/2 cup brown sugar
2 cups lukewarm water
2 Tbsp molasses
1/2 tsp salt
2 cups rye flour
2 cups white flour

MAKES 4 LOAVES

SWEDISH RYE BREAD
Saint Libory

"We have recipes passed down from my grandma Nellie Larson that can't be beat," writes Pat Frauen of Saint Libory. *"Of course, none of us can make it like her, but we try. This has been passed down and passed around to all our descendants."*

Dissolve yeast in 1/2 cup warm water before adding 1 tsp granulated sugar. Add this to the 2 cups lukewarm water and 2 cups white flour. Beat well and set aside in a warm place to rise. Batter will be sticky. When doubled, add molasses, brown sugar, butter, salt and rye flour. Knead until soft and supple, about 10 minutes, using white flour to prevent sticking. Let rise about 1 hour and divide dough into 4 parts. Grease and flour 4 pans, placing dough evenly in pans. Let dough rise until doubled. Bake at 350° for 45 minutes.

CORNBREAD FOR TWO & WILD PLUM SYRUP
Hyannis

1/2 cup cornmeal
1/2 cup flour
1 Tbsp sugar
2 tsp baking powder
1/4 tsp salt (optional)
1/2 cup milk
1 egg, lightly beaten
1/8 cup canola oil
1 6-inch iron

SERVES 2

SYRUP
　　Wild fruit
　　Sugar
　　Sure-Jell

"For health and an addition to their diets, wild fruit was very important to the Indians and pioneers," writes Ginger Fouse of Hyannis. *"As a child growing up in Custer County, summer days found me going with my grandmother to the canyons or shelter belts for buffalo berries, chokecherries or wild plums. In the fall it was off to the river for wild grapes. On days we made jell (grandma never called it jelly) we always had a huge skillet of corn bread with still-warm jell for supper. When I first learned to make this we fried a couple of slices of bacon and poured the grease into the batter."*

Mix dry ingredients and add milk and lightly-beaten egg. Stir until well-mixed. Pour oil in skillet and heat, swishing oil to coat sides of skillet. Pour batter into skillet which should be hot enough to make batter sizzle. That will make the bread crust come out of the pan in a perfect round shape to serve. Bake at 400° for 20 minutes.

WILD FRUIT SYRUP
Wash fruit and cook. Push through a colander to remove skins and seeds. Use juice with pulp for better flavor. Add 1 ¾ cup sugar to every 1 ¼ cup juice. Add 1 package Sure-Jell. Bring to a boil and boil exactly 1 minute 30 seconds. This recipe works for most berries and wild fruit.

SAUSAGE AND PECAN CORNBREAD
Wakefield

"This recipe is probably from when I lived down South," said Caroline Gordon of Wakefield. "I lived in Mobile, Ala., for ten years before moving back home to Nebraska in 1956."

Brown the pork sausage separately in pieces and drain off drippings. Sift together cornmeal, flour, sugar and baking powder. Add egg, milk and oil. Mix thoroughly and fold in sausage and pecans. Turn batter into a greased 9-inch glass pie plate. Bake at 400° for 30 minutes.

1	lb fresh pork sausage
1	cup yellow cornmeal
1/3	cup coarsely chopped pecans
4	tsp baking powder
1	egg
1	cup flour
1/4	cup sugar
1	cup milk
2	Tbsp oil

SERVES 6

Gramma Annie's
Caramel Cinnamon Rolls

"EVERYONE'S GRANDMA HAS SPECIAL TRAITS and relationships with their children's children," writes Rhonda McMurtry of Blair. "My father's mother lived on a farm and she took us fishing when she wasn't preparing large family meals.

"My mother's mother lived on an acreage with fruit trees and gardens of flowers, strawberries, asparagus, radishes, string beans, peas, carrots and lots of other vegetables. My mother was the crafter and historian. She let the grandkids help her redecorate her home and would tell stories of her family.

"My husband's mother was a tiny, independent woman who raised and supported her family by herself. Every one called her Gramma Annie. Even the postman knew where to deliver mail addressed to Gramma Annie in Craig. She lived in a small house on the edge of a small town and fed anything that crossed her property. She fed her children's friends, her children's pets and any stray creature that cried on her doorstep. And they all continued to return as Gramma Annie was a good cook.

"My daughter Carrie liked to cook, too, and they spent time together trying new recipes or baking old favorites like Gramma Annie's cinnamon rolls. College kids brought her flour so she would bake the rolls for them. The recipe was not written in any cookbook, just etched in Gramma's mind.

One chilly day, Rhonda McMurtry's 13-year-old daughter Carrie captured 'Gramma Annie's' cinnamon roll recipe and personality on a little green note pad.

"One chilly day (you always baked when it was cold so the oven could help heat the house), Carrie, then 13 years old, decided to write it down. She borrowed a green note pad that was two inches by four inches and wrote down everything that she and her grandmother did. She filled 12 pages and what follows is that recipe and some things that Carrie remembers from that day:

Gramma's Definitions

Big bowl: The largest green plastic bowl Grandma has in her kitchen

Flour thing: Flour canister

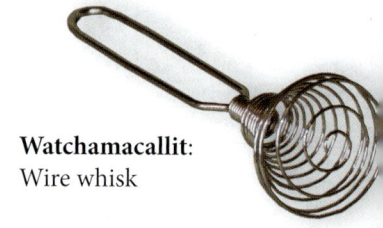

Watchamacallit: Wire whisk

From Carrie's note pad:

Make sure you have <u>lots</u> of flour.

Boil 4 cups of water (2 cups for a little wad). Get out <u>big</u> bowl. Put 4 tablespoons of lard, butter, oil or shortening in bowl. Pour water over whatever you put in bowl and let cool.

Stir in 1/2 cup sugar with whatchamacallit. Add 3 packages of yeast and stir with whatchamacallit. Wait until bubbles come up. Go out and talk to somebody. Add flour until it is thick making a light sponge. Stir with the whatchamacallit until all lumps are gone. Cover and let it set until it is fluffy. Refill flour thing.

Put lid some place so cat doesn't lay on it. Add flour to stuff until it is so thick you can't stir it with the whatchamacallit. Put flour on the counter. Put dough on flour. Put bowl somewhere so the cat doesn't get to it. Put whatchamacallit in the sink – you are finished with it!

Knead the dough, adding flour, until the dough is soft and not sticking to counter, but little sticky to touch. Put oil in bowl and mix it all around. Put dough back in bowl. Flip it so the side that has oil on it is up and put lid on it. Let it rise in a warm place until it lifts the lid – if you use a lid.

Get out a pan for the goop. Melt 2 cups brown sugar and 1 cup butter on the stove with a wooden spoon. Stir in 4 tablespoons corn syrup. Make cinnamon-sugar. Check dough. Change channel to 6 for Marsha Warfield and "Golden Girls." Get pans out of old, cluttered cabinet. Spoon 1 spoonful into each pan until all goop is gone. Spread with a spatula on the bottom of the pan. Scrape goop pan.

Get out butter and rolling pin. Get dough out and divide into four parts. Put a little flour on counter. Put first dough part on flour, then flip and roll out so it is about 10 inches by 12 inches. Smear butter on dough with doohickey. Shake cinnamon-sugar on buttered dough. Roll up dough. Pinch ends and the edge of dough. Divide roll in half, then each half into half. Divide the fourths into thirds. Put the rolls into the pan three by four. Put pan into oven and do other three parts of dough. Let the rolls grow until they touch each other.

Take them out and preheat the oven to 375-400°. Set dingy for 25 minutes. Yell for electricity. Sit and shiver. Let rolls cook until golden brown. First batch 25-30 minutes. Second batch 20-25 minutes. When done, remove from oven and set on counter. Put others in. Put foil on a cookie sheet. Put cookie sheet and foil on pan. Flip it all. Scrape goop off bottom and put on rolls. Put water in pans. Extra goop will get <u>really</u> hard. Let cool for awhile and eat.

To make Grandma's buns, (rolls have goop, buns just the cinnamon) do exactly the same thing only don't add the goop and bake 12-15 minutes at 400°.

2-4	cups boiling water
4	Tbsp butter, shortening, lard or vegetable oil
1/2	cup granulated sugar
3	package yeast
6-8	cups flour
2	cups brown sugar
1	cup butter
4	Tbsp corn syrup
1	cup granulated sugar
1-2	Tbsp cinnamon
	Soft butter for spreading

Makes 24 rolls

Goop: Caramel sauce to glaze rolls

Goop pan: saucepan used to make caramel

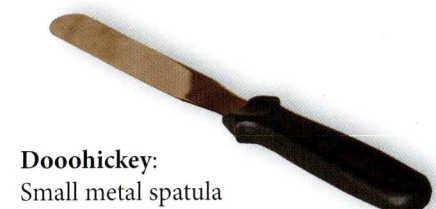

Dooohickey: Small metal spatula

Dingy: Kitchen timer

CRAISIN SALAD, PG. 26

CREAMY WHITE CHILI, PG. 30

GRANDMA'S PORK AND BEAN SALAD, PG. 33

BAKED STEW, PG. 39

Soups & Salads

In 1979 my husband and our family moved off the farm.
We owned and operated Sudbeck Service in Bow Valley for 19 years.
Many, many hamburgers, fries and fresh donuts were served.
We had a lot of feed meetings and suppers, sometimes serving over
100 people. We have sold our business and are now able to spend more
time with our children and their families. When everyone is together
we now have around 30 at our table. What a blessing.

– Janice Sudbeck

1   head romaine lettuce
1   cup grated Swiss
    cheese
1   cup craisins
    (dried cranberries)
1   cup salted cashews
1   pear, diced
1   apple, diced

DRESSING
1/2   cup sugar
1/3   cup lemon juice
2   tsp green onion,
     chopped finely
2/3   cup oil
1   tsp Dijon mustard
1/2   tsp salt
1   Tbsp poppy seeds

SERVES 8-10

CRAISIN SALAD
Newburgh, Ind.

"I claim Clearwater as home but have lived all over the country and many places in Nebraska," writes Lavona Reiss of Newburgh, Ind. "This salad is very tasty and attractive to serve. Friends from Nebraska have found me wherever I live and we always make it a 'Nebraska Day' when we can gather with food and fellowship."

Mix salad ingredients. Mix dressing ingredients, pour over salad and serve.

1/3   cup vinegar
3/4   cup sugar
1   small onion,
     quartered
1/2   tsp salt
1/2   tsp ground mustard
1   cup salad oil
2-4   tsp poppy seeds

MAKES 2 ½ CUPS

POPPY SEED AND ONION SALAD DRESSING
Scotia

"I enjoy making this delicious salad dressing," writes Phyllis Cargill of Scotia. "It is good on everything: pasta, leafy greens, spinach. It's our favorite."

In a blender, process until smooth vinegar, sugar, onion, salt and mustard. Gradually add salad oil, pouring a thin stream from the top to incorporate the mixtures. Add poppy seeds and pulse to mix. Dress salad immediately.

CREAMY CLAM CHOWDER

Syracuse

"This is one of my favorites to fill up two teen boys on a winter day," writes Karen Johnston of Syracuse. *"I usually double this and leave it going all day in the crock pot while I'm at work. I have substituted a can of corn when I didn't have the second can of cream corn, and it is just as good and creamy."*

Combine all ingredients in crock pot. Cook on medium for 3 hours or on low for 6 hours.

1 can cream corn
1 can potato soup
1 can half and half
1 small can minced clams, drained and rinsed
6 strips crispy bacon, crushed

SERVES 6

POTATO CHEESE SOUP

Falls City

"This is one of my favorite recipes and I love to share it with others," writes Ruth Heinzelman of Falls City. *"We can't wait for soup weather to make this."*

In large saucepan, place potatoes, carrots, celery, onion, salt and pepper in boiling water. Cover and cook 10 minutes to tenderize. Do not drain. In large saucepan or soup pot, melt butter.
   As butter bubbles, add flour, stirring constantly until flour is thoroughly blended and begins to turn golden. Gradually stir in milk. Continue to cook and stir until mixture thickens to make a sauce.
   Remove from heat and stir in the cheese, mixing until cheese melts. Add ham and cooked vegetables with their liquid. Heat if necessary to bring soup to serving temperature. Serve immediately.

2 cups boiling water
2 cup diced potatoes
1/2 cup diced carrots
1/2 cup diced celery
1/4 cup chopped onion
1 tsp salt
1/4 tsp pepper
1/4 cup butter
1/4 cup flour
2 cup milk
2 cups (8 oz) sharp cheddar cheese
1 cup cubed ham

SERVES 6-8

1 6-oz package grape
  or blackberry Jell-O
1 can blueberry pie
  filling
1 20-oz can crushed
  pineapple and juice
2 cups hot water

TOPPING
1 8-oz cream cheese,
  softened
1 can sour cream, at
  room temperature
1/2 cup sugar
4 tsp vanilla

SERVES 12-16

BLUEBERRY SALAD
North Platte

"I've had this for years," writes Arlene Knoll of Knoll's Country Inn Bed and Breakfast at North Platte. "I probably got it at some family gathering or another, probably from my sister-in-law. I like it because it's so easy to make."

Mix Jell-O with blueberry pie filling, pineapple and water in a 9 x 13-inch dish. Chill in refrigerator until firm. Mix topping ingredients in small bowl. Spread topping over set salad. Chill in refrigerator until topping is firm.

CHRISTMAS SALAD
Hastings

1 14-oz can sweetened
  condensed milk
3/4 cup lemon juice
1 20-oz can crushed
  pineapple, drained
1 16-oz can whole
  cranberry sauce
1/2 cup pecans, chopped
1 8-oz container
  whipped topping

SERVES 9-12

"I made this years ago and the family loved it," writes Ruth Janssen of Hastings. "They have the final say in any recipe I keep and make again. I found this around Christmas time, hence the title for 'Christmas Salad,' but I also make it throughout the year for other occasions. It can also be a light, cool dessert for summer, and you can use low fat ingredients to be light on calories."

In large bowl combine milk, lemon juice, pineapple, cranberry sauce and pecans. Mix thoroughly. Gently fold in whipped topping. Pour into 9 x 13-inch pan and freeze for several hours. Remove from freezer about 5 minutes before serving. Serve on a lettuce leaf with a small dollop of mayo or whipped topping and sprinkle with green decorator's sugar.

LADY BIRD'S CHILI
Fremont

"When I was in Austin, Texas, I found this recipe," writes Martha J. Warehime of Fremont. *"This was a favorite of President and Mrs. Johnson, their family and friends. It was served at the Texas White House and on board Air Force One. This is a chili without any beans."*

Brown meat, onion and garlic in a pan. Add oregano, cumin, chili powder, tomatoes, salt to taste and hot water. Bring to a boil. Lower heat and simmer for about an hour. As fat cooks out, skim off.

4   lbs ground beef
1   large onion, chopped
1   tsp oregano
1   tsp cumin
6   tsp chili powder
    (to taste)
2   cloves garlic, minced
2   1-lb can tomatoes,
    not drained
2   cups hot water
    Salt to taste

SERVES 8-10

1   Tbsp vegetable oil
1   medium onion,
    chopped
1   15-oz can garbanzo
    beans
2   15-oz cans great
    northern beans
1   15-oz can lima beans
1   15-oz can corn
1   14-oz can chicken
    broth
1   lb grilled or boiled
    chicken
1   4-oz can green
    chilies
1   tsp cumin
1   tsp salt
1   tsp pepper
1 ½ cups sour cream
1   cup half and half

SERVES 10-12

CREAMY WHITE CHILI
Edgar

"I have taken this for church soup dinner and everyone wanted the recipe," writes
Deloris Springer of Edgar. "You may substitute any beans of your liking."

In a large pan, heat the oil and sauté onions. Add beans, cooked chicken, broth,
corn, chilies, salt and pepper and cumin. Bring to a boil. Reduce heat and simmer
for 30 minutes uncovered. Remove from heat and stir in sour cream and half and
half. Return to heat on low, stirring constantly until reheated.

SHRIMP MACARONI SALAD

Loup City

"I am a sucker for salads, and macaroni salad was one of my favorites growing up," writes Tami Kuehl of Loup City. *"This is like a grown-up version with the cauliflower, green onions and black olives. You may substitute diced chicken or turkey for the shrimp."*

Cook and drain macaroni. Place in large bowl and toss with French dressing. Chill one hour. After chilling, stir in cauliflower pieces, onions, salt, pepper, shrimp and olives. In a separate bowl blend mayonnaise and chili sauce. Pour over pasta mixture. Toss and serve.

4	cups large uncooked shell macaroni
1/2	cup French dressing
2	cups raw cauliflower, cut into bite-sized pieces
1	cup sliced green onions
1/2	tsp salt
1/4	tsp pepper
2	5-oz cans medium shrimp, drained
1	cup sliced black olives, drained
1	cup mayonnaise
1/2	cup chili sauce

SERVES 6

CORN AND TOMATO SALAD

Palmer, Alaska

"Growing up in St. Helena, Neb, we will always be Cornhusker fans," writes Shari Kitchin of Palmer, Alaska. *"This is my 'Go Big Red' dish I take everywhere."*

Cook sweet corn until tender (about 5 minutes) in a large pot of boiling water. Drain and cool to room temperature. Cut kernels from ears and transfer to large bowl. Add remaining ingredients and mix well. Salt and pepper to taste. Serve immediately, or refrigerate for up to two hours.

6	medium ears sweet corn or bag of frozen corn
3	cups grape tomatoes, quartered
1/2	cup chopped red onion
4	Tbsp chopped cilantro
4	tsp extra virgin olive oil
4	Tbsp freshly squeezed lime juice, or 4 Tbsp rice wine vinegar
1/4	tsp ground cumin

SERVES 6

REGAL TOMATO SOUP
Norfolk

6 onions, chopped
1 bunch celery, chopped
8 quarts fresh tomatoes
1/4 cup salt
1 cup butter
1 cup flour
1 cup sugar

MAKES 10
PINT-SIZED JARS

"This is a great tomato soup when summer turns to fall," writes Carol Keating of Norfolk. "I used to make this all the time when I had a garden. When tomatoes are 'in' this is great way to use them up and enjoy them all winter long."

Chop the onion and celery and put in a large kettle with just enough water to start them cooking and keep them from burning. While the onions and celery simmer away, wash the tomatoes, cut out the white parts and stems, and measure out a good 8 quarts. Add these to the kettle and continue cooking until the celery and onions are tender and the tomatoes are cooked through.

Put the cooked vegetables and juice through a food mill to remove skins and vegetable chunks. Return this pulp and juice to the kettle. Add to this pulp the sugar and salt. Cream together the butter and flour. When this is completely blended, add to the boiling hot pulp. Stir well and continue simmering until it thickens slightly. Cook it about as long as you would gravy. It thickens more as it cools. The color becomes rich and creamy.

Pour the boiling hot soup into hot, sterilized jars. Seal immediately. This seals and keeps very well with this "open kettle" method. However, if you want to go one step further in preserving the soup, process for 10 minutes at 5 pounds in a pressure canner (optional).

When ready to serve, open a jar of the concentrated tomato soup, put into a saucepan, add two pinches of baking soda, heat slightly, stir in an equal amount of milk and continue heating until desired temperature is reached for serving.

GRANDMA'S PORK AND BEAN SALAD
Columbus

2 cans pork and beans
2 peeled large Granny Smith apples, diced
2 unpeeled medium Jonathan apples, diced
1 onion, chopped
3 Tbsp vinegar
3 Tbsp brown sugar

SERVES 10-12

"This is my grandma's recipe," writes Ruth Borchers of Columbus. "She came over from Germany and didn't bring a cookbook. She made everything from what she had available and all her recipes were from memory which she passed down to my mother. We have had this recipe in the family since 1900. It's very simple, and I always enjoy it."

Drain the pork and beans. Mix brown sugar and vinegar well. Add apples, onion, sugar and vinegar mixture to beans and serve.

TRAILER TREAT STEW
Vista, Calif.

3	Tbsp butter or margarine
1	medium onion, chopped
1	pound frankfurters, quartered lengthwise
1	Tbsp all-purpose flour
1 ½	tsp chili powder
1	tsp salt
2	15-oz cans red kidney beans
1	can garbanzo beans
1	can yellow hominy
1	16-oz can diced tomatoes

SERVES 6-8

"I grew up in Winside and have been traveling ever since graduating from the University of Nebraska-Lincoln," writes Elsie L. Weible from Vista, Calif. "This stew was a favorite with a small group of 'RVers' who liked to spend their weekends away from telephones and yard work."

In large kettle or Dutch oven, sauté onion and frankfurters until lightly browned. Blend in flour, chili powder, salt, beans, tomatoes, beans and hominy. Simmer covered for 15 minutes.

OLD FASHIONED SWEET/SOUR COLE SLAW
Andover, Kan.

1 ½	lbs shredded green cabbage
1	tsp salt
2/3	cup sugar
1/3	cup apple vinegar
1	cup whipping cream

SERVES 6-8

"Thinking of my summers growing up in Spalding always remind me of our big garden and all the great food my mother would make with our harvest," writes Mary Lynn Dake of Andover, Kan. "This recipe for cole slaw was a favorite with me and my siblings."

Place shredded cabbage in covered dish in the refrigerator for several hours until thoroughly chilled. 30 minutes before serving, mix salt, sugar, vinegar and whipping cream in a medium-size bowl and refrigerate. Immediately before serving add cabbage to mixture and combine well.

MOSER'S POTATO SALAD

Sioux City, Iowa

"This is my mom's recipe. She made it when we went fishing or camping when I was growing up on our farm near Randolph. I try to make it now but it's never as good as hers," writes Larry Moser of Sioux City, Iowa.

Wash potatoes but do not peel. Bake at 350° for 1 hour. Place in refrigerator until cool. Peel and dice potatoes into small cubes. Dice hard boiled eggs. Mix eggs, potatoes and remaining ingredients in a large bowl. Place in refrigerator to cool again. For best results, leave potato salad in refrigerator overnight.

8-9	medium sized red potatoes
2	hard boiled eggs
1/4	medium white onion
1/2	cup Miracle Whip
1/4	cup milk
1	Tbsp sugar
1	tsp vinegar
1	tsp mustard
1/4	tsp salt
1/4	tsp pepper

SERVES 6-8

HOMEMADE SALAD DRESSING

Creighton

"This is truly a hand-me-down recipe," writes Carol Tyler of Creighton. *"This originally came from my mother, Myrtle Schlotes, who says it will keep up to a year in the refrigerator. We make a new batch so often we can't say for sure."*

In medium saucepan, combine eggs, sugar, water, mustard, vinegar, flour and salt. Whisk ingredients and cook until thick, stirring constantly. Thin with cream if necessary (or store-bought salad dressing).

4	eggs
1	cup sugar
1	cup water
2	tsp mustard
1	cup vinegar
4	Tbsp flour
2	tsp salt

MAKES 3 CUPS

1 box macaroni
3 cucumbers, diced
1 green pepper, diced
2 onions, chopped
1 jar pimento

DRESSING
3/4 cup oil
3/4 cup vinegar
3/4 cup sugar
1 can tomato soup

SERVES 6-8

MACARONI SALAD
Wilsonville

"This recipe is a family favorite with all my children," writes Dora Shaw of Wilsonville. *"You can use different types of macaroni – it's so good with spinach-tomato!"*

Cook macaroni according to package instructions. Drain and rinse in cold water. Dice cucumbers, green pepper, onions, and pimento and put in a large bowl with macaroni. Mix together dressing ingredients and pour all but one cup on macaroni mixture. Marinate overnight.

When ready to serve, pour remaining dressing on salad, then toss and serve.

3 lbs seedless grapes, stemmed
1/4 cup brown sugar
1 cup (8 oz) cream cheese
1 tsp vanilla
1 pint heavy cream, whipped

SERVES 8-10

GRAPE SALAD
Bow Valley

"I love cooking and I am always looking for new recipes," writes Janice Sudbeck of Bow Valley. *"This is one of my crowd pleasing salads."*

In serving bowl place washed and stemmed seedless grapes. In small mixing bowl beat brown sugar, cream cheese and vanilla until light and fluffy. In medium mixing bowl whip heavy cream until stiff peaks form. Fold cream cheese into whipped cream. Fold whipped cream mixture with grapes.

Ham & Macaroni Salad

Hastings

"Once I was making macaroni salad and had some leftover ham," writes Ronda Johnson of Hastings. *"I thought, 'Why not put them together?' It turned out great with the mustard flavor dressing. This is a crowd pleaser."*

In large stock pot boil 8-12 cups water. Cook macaroni according to package directions. Drain. In medium mixing bowl combine sugar, salt, relish, onion, mayonnaise and mustard. Mix well.

   Add green pepper, cheese and ham to dressing. In large serving bowl, combine pasta with dressing and ham. Mix thoroughly with rubber spatula so not to break macaroni. Chill for 6 hours.

4	cups uncooked macaroni
1/2	cup sugar
1/2	tsp salt
1/2	cup sweet pickle relish
1/2	cup chopped onion
2	cups mayonnaise
1/4	cup prepared mustard
1	green pepper, chopped
12	oz cheddar cheese, cubed
12	oz cubed ham

SERVES 16

Mountain Dew Salad

Atkinson

"This recipe is from my grandmother, Caroline Nansel," writes Claudeen Penry of Atkinson. *"She would bring this to all the family picnics. Over time she became diabetic and learned to cook without sugar. This recipe is perfectly suited to go sugar free. Just omit the marshmallows if you can't find sugar free ones."*

In a 9 x 13-inch pan, dissolve Jell-O in boiling water. Add Mountain Dew, bananas, marshmallows and pineapple. Refrigerate until set. Mix instant pudding as directed on package. Fold whipped topping into pudding and spread on top of mixture.

2	3-oz packages lemon Jell-O
2	cups boiling water
2	cups Mountain Dew
2	bananas, sliced
2	cups miniature marshmallows
1	cup crushed pineapple, drained
1	8-oz container frozen whipped topping
1	3-oz package instant lemon pudding Milk as directed for lemon pudding

SERVES 8-12

PINEAPPLE SALAD
Whitman

1 large can crushed pineapple
1 cup sugar
1 3-oz package orange Jell-O
1 cup grated Velveeta cheese
1 cup heavy cream, whipped
1/2 cup chopped walnuts

SERVES 6-8

"My mother was a wonderful cook who made everything from scratch and never used recipes," writes Phyllis Phillips of Whitman. *"Consequently, my sisters and I don't have many heirloom recipes. The following is one of the few recipes she used. I thought it was delicious then, and still do. The cheese gives it a unique taste and keeps people guessing about the ingredients."*

In medium sauce pan, bring pineapple and sugar to boil, stirring until slightly thickened. Add Jell-O and stir until dissolved. Pour into large mixing bowl and let cool. Add cheese, fold in whipped cream and nuts. Pour into 9 x 13-inch dish. Chill until firm.

PEAR SALAD
Grand Island

1 3 oz package lemon Jell-O
1 16-20 oz can of pears (drain and reserve juice)
8 oz cream cheese, softened
8 oz whipped topping, thawed

SERVES 8-10

"We have such a large family that we need several reunions to get everyone together," writes Leora Kuhlmann of Grand Island. *"We all trade our recipes at our reunions. This recipe came from my husband Jerry's stepmother. It has been a family favorite; it's so creamy and delicious, and so easy to make."*

Heat 1 cup of pear juice to boiling. Dissolve Jell-O in juice. Combine Jell-O mixture, pears and cream cheese in blender. Whip until smooth. Let cool. Fold the whipped topping into the mixture and pour into a mold or pan. Refrigerate to set.

Baked Stew

Loup City

"This recipe came from my grandmother Barbara Gordon and I finally tried it many years after she passed on," writes Tami Kuehl of Loup City. "It has become a favorite, especially during the cold, windy and snowy days in Nebraska. Rest assured, Grandma, we're thinking of you every time we cook up a big batch of this baked stew."

Chop stew meat into bite-sized pieces and place in large oven-proof pot that has been sprayed with non-stick cooking spray. Dice onion, celery, potatoes and carrots; add to stew meat. Add remaining ingredients to meat and vegetables; stir to combine.

Cover pot and bake at 250° for 5 hours. Do not lift the lid or brown the meat. You can substitute canned tomatoes for the soup. A crockpot on high power also works well.

2	lbs stew meat
1	large onion
1	cup celery
6-8	medium potatoes
2	cups carrots
2	Tbsp instant tapioca granules
1	clove garlic
1	10 ¾-oz can tomato soup, undiluted
2/3	cup water
1	Tbsp sugar
1	Tbsp salt
1	tsp pepper

Serves 6

All Occasion Salad

Austin, Minn.

"I came upon this salad recipe stuck in a drawer when I wanted something a little different for our family reunions," writes Selene Shuster Schultz of Austin, Minn. "Born in Denman, Neb., I have fond memories of the general store, but I call Fremont my home after living in seven small Nebraska towns. This is just one of my favorite Nebraska recipes that brings back so many memories."

In a large serving bowl, combine salad greens and cauliflower. Mix sugar and mayo for the dressing. Toss salad with dressing just before serving. Top with Parmesan cheese and bacon bits.

2	bags mixed salad greens (or create your own like the original recipe instructed)
1	head cauliflower, cut into small pieces
1	cup real mayonnaise
1/2	cup sugar
1	lb bacon, cooked crisp, drained and broken into pieces
1	cup Parmesan cheese

Serves 6-8

4   cups bite-size fresh
    broccoli florettes
3   Tbsp red onion
2   Tbsp dried
    cranberries
3/4 cup Jimmy's cole
    slaw dressing

SERVES 8

BROCCOLI SUPREME SALAD
Lincoln

"I just found this easy-to-make, no-fuss recipe lately," writes Ethel Krull of Lincoln. "I take it to my clubs and gatherings. It is better the next day and keeps for several days."

Combine all ingredients and add the cole slaw dressing. Refrigerate overnight.

1   cup chopped green
    pepper
1   cup sliced celery
1/2 cup sliced green onion
2   Tbsp diced pimento
1   16-oz can cut green
    beans, drained
1   12-oz can corn,
    drained
1   10-oz package
    frozen peas
1/2 cup sugar
1/2 tsp salt
1/2 cup cider vinegar
1/8 cup canola oil
    Pepper to taste

SERVES 6-8

WONDERFUL VEGETABLE SALAD
Fremont

Ellen Bonsall of Fremont sends the following recipe and writes, "This vegetable salad is one of my husband's favorites. Hope you enjoy it!"

In large serving bowl, combine green pepper, celery, onion, pimento, green beans, corn and peas. In small mixing bowl, combine sugar, salt, pepper, vinegar and oil. Whisk together and pour over vegetables. Cover and marinate overnight before serving.

CRANBERRY-TURKEY SALAD
Wakefield

"Looking for ways to use the Thanksgiving leftovers, I came across this recipe," writes Caroline Gordon of Wakefield. "This was a favorite I made when the kids were still at home."

In a medium bowl, combine turkey, apple pieces, raisins and walnuts. In a small bowl, mix cranberry sauce with orange juice. Set aside. In salad bowls or plates arrange lettuce leaves. Top each with 1 cup salad mix and garnish with kiwifruit. Drizzle with cranberry-orange sauce.

2	cups cooked turkey, cubed
1	large red apple, cored and cut up into bite-size pieces
1/4	cup raisins
2	Tbsp walnuts, coarsely chopped
1	can jellied cranberry sauce
1/4	tsp orange juice concentrate
2	small heads bibb lettuce, torn in small pieces
2	kiwifruit, peeled and sliced

SERVES 4-6

LIMA STEW WITH MEATBALLS
Austin, Minn.

"Bob and Joan Frazee were our neighbors on East 20th Street in Fremont," writes Selene Schuster Schulz of Austin, Minn. "Bob and Joan were the best friends a person could have. Because Bob and Joan were raising six children on a tight budget, Joan would find recipes that would feed a crowd at a reasonable price. Oftentimes, she would call us to come over and try her 'new' dishes with them."

Rinse beans. Place in Dutch oven; add water and boil two minutes. Cover; let stand one hour (or soak beans overnight without cooking). Do not drain. Combine flour and cold water. Stir into beans; cook until thickened and bubbly. Add vegetables, bay leaf and 2 tsp salt. Bring to boil.

Cover and bake at 375° for 1 hour 30 minutes, stirring occasionally. Combine bread crumbs, remaining salt, milk and Worcestershire sauce; mix into ground beef. Shape into small meatballs. Add to stew.

Cover and continue baking for 45 minutes. Remove bay leaf.

1	cup large dry lima beans
4 ½	cups water
1/2	cup water
1/4	cup all purpose flour
1	8-oz can diced tomatoes
1	cup sliced celery
1	cup sliced carrots
1/2	cup chopped onions
1	bay leaf
2 ½	tsp salt
1/4	cup dried bread crumbs
1/4	cup milk
1/4	tsp Worcestershire sauce
1	lb ground beef

SERVES 6

Breakfast at the Villa

Three Recipes from Pam Halsey

PAM AND DANE HALSEY have become breakfast experts since starting their Tuscan Villa Bed & Breakfast in the hills west of Pierce. Here are a few of their favorite recipes.

Pam Halsey, right, with Sarah's fruit pizza.

1	tube refrigerated sugar cookie dough
1	8-oz package cream cheese, softened
1/2	cup sugar
1	tsp vanilla
4	Tbsp cornstarch
1	cup pineapple juice
1/2	cup sugar
1	tsp lemon juice
	Strawberries, sliced
	Kiwifruit, sliced
	Blueberries
	Grapes
	Pineapple, drained, reserving juice
	Mandarin oranges, drained

Serves 8-12

SARAH'S FRUIT PIZZA

"When cooking for our guests, I often use many recipes from fellow members of our church family. This one is from Sarah Bruce."

Press and roll onto a baking dish or cookie sheet the sugar cookie dough. Bake at 350° for 7-11 minutes, or until golden brown. Let cool. In a small mixing bowl combine cream cheese, sugar and vanilla; mix well and spread over cooled cookie. Decorate with cut-up of pieces of fruit, reserving some fruit for garnish.

In medium saucepan, combine cornstarch, pineapple juice, sugar, and lemon juice. Cook until thick, stirring constantly. Pour cooled glaze over fruit and refrigerate. Top with extra-large strawberries or other reserved fruits.

Pumpkin Nut Belgian Waffles

"These waffles taste like fresh-baked pumpkin pie. Our guests love them."

Combine first ingredients in medium size bowl. Combine second ingredients in larger bowl and mix well. Add dry ingredients to canned pumpkin in large bowl and mix thoroughly with wire whisk until smooth. In third bowl, whip egg whites until stiff peaks form. Gently fold egg whites into pumpkin batter. Pour mixture into waffle iron. Serve with real maple syrup or flavored syrups, whipped topping and any kind of fresh fruit.

First Bowl

1 ½   cups flour
1/8   cup (1 oz) finely chopped pecans
1   Tbsp cornstarch
1   Tbsp baking powder
1   tsp salt
1 ¾   tsp pumpkin pie spice

Second Bowl

3/4   cup canned pumpkin
3   eggs separated (yolks for the second bowl) and (whites in separate third bowl)
1   cup whole milk
1/4   cup real maple syrup (do not use pancake syrup)
3   Tbsp melted butter
1   tsp vanilla extract
Real maple syrup
Whipped topping
Flavored syrups
Fresh fruit

Makes 6
LARGE WAFFLES

Pecan Nut French Toast

"This is a great recipe for an in-a-hurry/no-fuss breakfast. When you need to take it easy or catch a few more winks of sleep, you can count on this recipe to make breakfast worth having."

Place sliced French or Italian bread in a shallow baking dish so sides can touch but are not overlapping. In a large pouring bowl, mix together eggs, sugar, nutmeg, orange juice and vanilla. Pour egg mixture over the bread slices. Cover and refrigerate overnight. The following morning spray a cookie or baking sheet with cooking spray.

Preheat oven to 400°. Put stick of butter on baking sheet and melt in oven 5-10 minutes. After butter has melted, lay egg-saturated bread on baking sheet. Bake at 400° for 10-15 minutes. Remove from oven and turn over slices. Sprinkle with finely chopped pecans and bake an additional 15-20 minutes. Remove from oven and serve with powdered sugar, whipped topping, fresh fruit and flavored syrups.

12-15   slices of Italian or French bread, sliced thick
6   large eggs
1/4   cup sugar
1/2   tsp fresh ground nutmeg
1   cup orange juice
1   tsp vanilla
1/2   cup butter (1 stick)
Chopped pecans
Powdered sugar
Whipped topping
Fresh fruit
Flavored syrups

SERVES 12-15

Pork Roast with Parsnips, pg. 51

Myrna's Meatloaf, pg. 57

ASHLEY'S TATOR TOT BRUNCH CASSEROLE, PG. 53

INDIAN TACO, PG. 65

Main Dishes

Even though my grandparents had 10 children and were
not wealthy people, they took in others in need. On Sundays,
the married children and their families would come to the
family farm to eat together. That tradition carried on to the next
generation and the next generation. No matter how much or
little money we had in our home while growing up, food
was meant to be shared with those you love.

– *Selene Shuster Schulz*

Square Eggs
Omaha

7 eggs, slightly beaten
1 cup cottage cheese
8 oz grated cheddar or longhorn cheese
1/2 cup melted butter or margarine
1 cup Bisquick

Serves 8

"We got this recipe from our daughter-in-law Christine Cook many years ago," writes Ruth Cook of Omaha. *"Sometimes we call them 'square eggs' because we cut them in squares when serving."*

In a large bowl combine eggs, cottage cheese, 1/2 cup cheese, butter and Bisquick. Pour egg mixture into a greased 9 x 13-inch glass pan. Sprinkle remaining cheese on top. Bake at 350° for 40-45 minutes or until golden brown.

CHICKEN FILLED CORN PUFFS

Wilber

"I love to make cream puffs," writes Carol Fictum of Wilber. *"Although they are known as a dessert, this variation is used as a main dish with a creamed chicken filling."*

Combine cornmeal, flour, onion powder and salt. Set aside. In a medium saucepan, add water and butter. Bring to a rolling boil. Stir in cornmeal mixture; stir well over low heat just until mixture forms a ball, cleaning sides of pan. Remove from heat. Beat in eggs, cold from the refrigerator, one at a time until mixture is smooth. Drop 1/4 cup onto un-greased baking sheet. Bake until puffed, golden and crisp, about 30-40 minutes at 400°. Do not open oven door during baking.

Drain corn, reserving liquid. Add enough milk to corn liquid to measure 1¾ cups. Set aside. In a medium saucepan, melt butter over low heat. Whisk in flour, chili powder, mustard, seasoning, salt and pepper. Gradually stir in milk and corn liquid. Cook and stir until thickened.

    Add chicken, peas, pimento and corn. Mix and reheat. Cut off the tops of cooled puffs and set aside. Pull out soft dough and fill with hot chicken filling. Replace tops and serve.

PUFFS

1/3	cup cornmeal
3	eggs
1/3	cup flour
1 ½	tsp onion powder
1/4	tsp salt
1/3	cup butter or margarine
3/4	cup water

MAKES 6 CORN PUFFS

FILLING

1	8-oz can whole kernel corn
3	Tbsp butter or margarine
1/4	cup flour
1/2	tsp chili powder
1/4	tsp dry mustard
1/2	tsp seasoned salt
2	cups cooked chicken, diced
3/4	cup cooked frozen peas
2	Tbsp chopped pimento
	Milk
	Salt and pepper

MAKES 4 CUPS

1	lb eye of round steak
1	can tomato sauce
1	can beef broth
3	Tbsp olive oil
2-4	Tbsp soy sauce
1/4	cup cornstarch
2	cups white rice, cooked
	Salt and pepper
	Dash of sugar (maybe 1/4 tsp)
	Green, red and yellow peppers, sliced in lengthwise strips

SERVES 4-6

PEPPER STEAK
Norfolk

"My mother Jan Arkfeld made this recipe quite often but never wrote it down," writes Angela Amundson of Norfolk. "I have adapted this recipe by using tomato sauce instead of tomato juice and omitting the ginger. It is a quick and easy recipe, but you need to taste it as you go for saltiness as amounts are not exact. My mom always tasted as she cooked, and everything she made was delicious."

Slice meat into 1/4-inch strips. Heat olive oil in large skillet. Brown meat with diced onions, soy sauce, salt and pepper. Add beef broth, tomato sauce and a dash of sugar (just to cut acidity of tomatoes). Cook on medium heat for 10-15 minutes.

Add sliced peppers. Cook until peppers are heated through or done to your likeness. In a small bowl add cornstarch and small amount of cold water to liquefy. Pour into skillet and stir to thicken sauce with the meat and peppers. Serve over rice.

3	lbs beef
2	lbs pork
2	cups milk
8	eggs
2	cups bread crumbs
1/4	cup onion, finely chopped or ground
2 ½	Tbsp salt
1	tsp pepper

MAKES 90 MEDIUM-SIZED MEATBALLS

SWEDISH MEATBALLS
Hooper

"My mother Elsie Eckerson came to the United States from Sweden," writes Audrey Eckerson Hansen of Hooper. "These are her tried-and-true Swedish meatballs made the old fashioned way using a meat grinder. You can ask your local butcher to grind the meats together. Usually they will."

Grind meats together three times. In a large bowl, mix milk and eggs. Add bread crumbs and let milk mixture soak into bread. Add meat to soaked bread crumbs and mix by hand.

Add onion, salt and pepper, working by hand until light and fluffy. Form meatballs the size of a walnut. Sauté meatballs in large skillet on medium heat. Turn meatballs as they brown.

GYPSY SPAGHETTI
Gainesville, Ga.

"This unusual one-dish meal was often served by my mother Phyllis Shallcross," writes Mary Jirik of Gainesville, Ga. *"Mom was born and raised in Bellevue, went to University of Nebraska-Lincoln and went back to Bellevue where she stayed, raised the family and got involved in her community."*

Cook bacon in large skillet. When crisp, pour off one-third of the grease and add onions and green pepper. Brown slightly and add tomato juice. Bring to a boil. Add uncooked spaghetti and cook 20 minutes or until mixture is thickened. Reduce heat to simmer. Cover and stir two to three times while cooking.

1/2 lb bacon, sliced into bite-size pieces
2 medium onions, sliced
1 green pepper, chopped
3 cups tomato juice
1 ½ cups broken spaghetti
Salt and pepper to taste

SERVES 6-8

BAKED ROUND STEAK
Norfolk

"This was a family favorite when I was growing up – one my dad would make when he had to cook because my mom was working a different shift than he was," writes Carol Keating of Norfolk. *"When my children were growing up, it was also their favorite with fresh, creamy mashed potatoes. I could put it in the oven before we went to church and it would be done when we got home. It is still a family favorite and my children are now cooking it for their families, but in the crock pot."*

Cut steak into serving-size pieces and coat with flour that has been seasoned with salt and pepper. Brown meat in shortening. Put browned steak into roasting pan or crock pot. Combine and mix soup with milk, then pour over steak. Bake at 300° for 2 hours or 4-6 hours in crock pot on low setting.

To make gravy, remove steak from roaster and add milk to soup remaining in pan.

1 package round steak, tenderized
1 cup flour
2 Tbsp shortening
1 can cream of mushroom soup
1 soup can milk
Salt and pepper to taste

SERVES 4-6

1　5-6 lb beef brisket
2-4　Tbsp A-1 steak sauce
2-4　Tbsp liquid smoke
2-4　Tbsp Worcestershire
　　　sauce
　　　Garlic powder to
　　　taste
　　　Coarse pepper to
　　　taste
　　　Seasoned salt to taste

SERVES 8-10

SUE'S OVEN-SMOKED BEEF BRISKET
Harrison

"I grew up in Harrison where my great-grandfather C. F. Coffee founded our Hatcreek Ranch in 1873," writes Ann Wackman of Brenham, Texas. "Beef production there has been our family's livelihood ever since. In fact, I was the Nebraska Stockgrounds Queen in 1968, a position that was primarily for the promotion of beef."

"Now whenever our family gathers at the ranch for brandings or other occasions, my sister's beef brisket is on the menu. It feeds a large group of people and it is tender and delicious."

Preheat oven to 300°. Line baking pan or lidded skillet with heavy-duty foil. With brisket "lean" side up, rub in dry seasonings generously. Turn brisket "fat" side up in lined baking pan. Pour on liquid seasonings and rub in more dry seasonings.

Close foil securely and place in oven, still "fat" side up. Reduce oven temperature to 250°. Roast 5-6 hours. Discard juices before serving.

1　chicken, cut up
1　egg
1/4　cup milk
1　cup flour
2　tsp garlic salt
1　tsp paprika
1/4　tsp poultry seasoning
　　　Vegetable shortening
　　　Ground pepper to
　　　taste

SERVES 8

CRISCO FRIED CHICKEN
Gordon

"The secret to great fried chicken is in the grease," writes Laveta Cole of Gordon. "My mother always used Crisco brand shortening so I always used Crisco. It makes the difference."

In shallow bowl combine the egg and milk. In another shallow bowl combine the flour, garlic salt, paprika, poultry seasoning and ground pepper. Dip the chicken pieces in the flour mixture first, coating all sides. Then dip the floured chicken pieces into the milk and egg batter. Return the egg-dipped chicken piece back into the flour.

When all pieces of the chicken are coated twice with flour, fry in skillet with melted vegetable shortening at 365° uncovered for about 10 minutes. After turning, reduce heat to 350°. Fry until golden brown and juices run clear.

PORK ROAST WITH PARSNIPS

Andover, Kan.

This recipe has been a favorite for 25 years in Mary Lynn Dake's family. A co-worker gave it to her when she moved as a newlywed from Spalding, Neb., to Kansas.

Place pork roast in center of roasting pan and season with salt and pepper. Combine marmalade and rosemary in small bowl. Spread half of mixture over pork roast. Add orange juice and olive oil to remaining marmalade mixture and reserve for the sauce.

   Toss parsnips and onions in marmalade mixture and place in roasting pan with roast. Cover and bake 25 minutes per pound at 350°, or approximately 2 hours 30 minutes. Remove roast and vegetables to serving platter. Add cornstarch to reserved marmalade mixture in small saucepan. Cook over medium heat until thickened. Pour over roast and vegetables before serving.

1   boneless pork roast
1   12-ounce jar orange marmalade
1   Tbsp rosemary
1   lb parsnips, peeled and cut into 3-inch pieces
2   medium onions, peeled and cut into 1-inch pieces
1/2 cup orange juice
1   Tbsp olive oil
1   Tbsp cornstarch
   Salt and pepper to taste

SERVES 6-8

3 lbs hamburger
2 cups oatmeal
2 eggs
1 cup chopped onion
1 13-oz can
  evaporated milk
2 tsp salt
1 tsp pepper
1/2 tsp garlic powder
2 tsp chili powder

SAUCE

2 cups ketchup
1 cup brown sugar
1/2 cup chopped onion
1/2 tsp garlic powder
2 tsp liquid smoke

MAKES 3-4 DOZEN
MEATBALLS

BARBECUE MEATBALLS
Pierce

"This is an old recipe that my daughter Diana acquired when she lived in Kansas. She is now back in Pierce, Neb.," writes Ruth Haller. "This recipe is simple and she makes it quite often, even for special occasions."

In large mixing bowl, combine hamburger, oatmeal, eggs, onion, evaporated milk, salt, pepper, garlic powder and chili powder. Mix thoroughly. Shape into balls and place in shallow baking dish, single layer. (Line pan with aluminum foil to make clean up easier.)

In mixing bowl, combine ketchup, brown sugar, onion, garlic powder and liquid smoke. Mix sauce and pour over meatballs. Bake uncovered at 350° for 1 hour.

STUFFED CHICKEN THIGHS
Hastings

Betty Cramton sends this favorite from Hastings:

"I was a farm wife for 42 years and took more meals to the field than I can begin to count. One harvest main dish that was always a favorite was my stuffed chicken thighs. Now 40-plus years later, it is still the one I use when I need something easy to transport and/or sure to impress. Recently I got an S.O.S. call from my sister-in-law who was cooking for the crew and needed the chicken recipe. She said it wouldn't be harvest without it!"

6-8 chicken thighs
6-8 package brown and
    serve sausage links,
    precooked

SEASONED FLOUR
1 cup flour
1/2 tsp salt
1/8 tsp pepper
  Oil for frying

SERVES 6-8

De-bone thighs (you can find the boneless/skinless variety in the freezer case). Replace the bone with a sausage link. Skewer the seam shut with a toothpick. Dredge in seasoned flour and fry until golden brown and juices run clear. Remove toothpicks before serving. Save the drippings for wonderful gravy.

ASHLEY'S TATOR TOT BRUNCH CASSEROLE

Hastings

"One Sunday morning my granddaughter Ashley and I were up early and decided to make an egg casserole for breakfast for everyone," writes Ronda Johnson of Hastings. *"I looked at my recipes and didn't have the hash browns I needed. I did find Tator Tots, so we created this casserole. Now it is the only one we make."*

Grease bottom of 9 x 13-inch pan and cover with Tator Tots. Bake according to package directions (about 20 minutes at 425°). When done, cover Tator Tots with cubed ham then cover with cheese. Beat eggs and sour cream well until light and airy. Pour over cheese. Bake at 350° for 35 minutes or until eggs are set and golden brown.

1	2-lb package Tator Tots
1 ½	cups cubed ham
1 ½	cups shredded cheddar cheese
3/4	cup sour cream
8	eggs

SERVES 8-12

4 cups diced chicken
1 can cream of celery soup
1 can of chicken soup
1 can chicken broth
2 cups noodles
1 small onion, diced
1/2 package Lipton onion soup mix
3/4 cups cheddar or Velveeta cheese
Buttered bread cubes

SERVES 6-8

LOIS' CHICKEN CASSEROLE
Deshler

"This is a good dish for using up leftover turkey," writes Lois Mueller of Deshler. "I have taken it to numerous potluck dinners and have been asked for the recipe often."

Cook noodles in chicken broth until tender. Drain and set aside. Mix all ingredients together, except the cheese and bread cubes. Add additional chicken broth if mixture is dry.

Spoon into a greased 8 x 10-inch casserole dish. Sprinkle with cheese. Top with buttered bread cubes. Refrigerate at least 1 hour before baking. Bake at 350° for 1 hour. Casserole may be made ahead and frozen.

Bobom's Zucchini Casserole
Sargent

3	medium-size zucchini
1	small onion
1 ½	lbs browned hamburger
1	package chicken Stove Top stuffing
1	cup sour cream
1	can chicken soup
1	cup grated carrots

SERVES 6-8

"This was given to me by my son-in-law Willie Hollaway," writes Fern Heitz of Sargent. "It was a special recipe from his grandmother Jane VanderBush."

Prepare stuffing according to directions on box. Brown and season hamburger then mix with sour cream and chicken soup. Skin onion and zucchini and cut into thin slices. Boil 5 minutes in small amount of water. Add carrots.

Pour hamburger-soup mixture into separate baking dish. Add half the stuffing, then a layer of the vegetables, then the remainder of the stuffing. Bake at 350° for 45-50 minutes.

Chicken Pie
Primrose

4	chicken breasts
5	Tbsp butter or margarine
1/4	cup chopped onion
5	Tbsp flour
1/8	tsp nutmeg
2	cup chicken stock
1/4	cup cream
1	3-oz can sliced mushrooms
1	tsp chicken soup base or cubed bouillon Salt and pepper to taste
1	uncooked pie crust

SERVES 4

"This is a recipe my mother used back when there was no electricity," writes Wilma West of Primrose. "There was no way to keep food refrigerated, so we had our chickens fresh and we depended a great deal on the chickens we kept at the farm. The recipe has changed to 4 chicken breasts instead of a 4 lb chicken. The mushrooms are an addition, and the poultry seasoning was used instead of soup base."

Boil chicken until tender and remove meat from bones. Reserve chicken stock for sauce.

In skillet, brown onion in butter until translucent. Add flour and nutmeg. Cook, stirring until smooth and bubbly.

Remove from heat, slowly stirring in stock and cream. Return to heat and cook until smooth. Add mushrooms, soup base or bouillon and cut-up chicken. Place in large casserole dish and cover with pie pastry. Bake at 400° for 15 minutes or until top is brown.

4 lbs beef tenderloin
6 cloves garlic
chopped course
1 can beer
1/2 bottle Worcestershire
sauce
Dash pepper and salt
to taste

SERVES 8-10

Chateau Briand
Colorado Springs, Colo.

"I was raised in Stratton and get my meat from Benkelman where my brother and his family live when I come to visit," writes Jerome Jones of Colorado Springs, Colo. "There's nothing like Nebraska beef! You can cut this meat with a fork. I'm a Cornhusker at heart and still consider myself a Nebraskan."

In a large bowl, mix garlic, beer and Worcestershire sauce. Trim meat. Marinate 5 hours, rotating hourly. Remove meat and place on grill over low flame, braze all over and then place on indirect heat.

For a wood smoker, use mesquite and apple wood chips, 50 percent each. Set on smoke for 3 hours. Open hood every 30 minutes and pour a little marinate over meat. Increase temperature to 475° and finish cooking. Remove meat and cover when internal temperature reaches 143°. Slice 3/4 inch thick and serve.

This can be done on a regular barbeque grill or in the oven at 350° for an hour or so as well.

1/4 cup canola oil (or
a mixture of canola
and Italian dressing)
2 Tbsp soy sauce
2 Tbsp lemon juice
1 Tbsp Worcestershire
sauce
1 tsp black pepper
1 dash cayenne pepper

MAKES MARINADE FOR
4-6 STEAKS

Maribel's Venison Marinade
Farwell

Maribel Bartels of Farwell sent this recipe:

"Since my husband took up deer hunting a decade ago I had to come up with a way to make the meat enjoyable for the entire family. Even our picky daughter will eat venison steaks if prepared with this marinade. I recommend using the grill to enhance the flavor and get the husband out of the house for a while!"

Mix ingredients in glass bowl. Place steaks in resealable plastic bag and pour in marinade. Lay bag flat in a cake pan and place in refrigerator with steaks flat in one layer. Marinate for 6 hours or longer, turning occasionally. Grill steaks to your preference and serve.

MYRNA'S MEATLOAF

Omaha

"This recipe originated with my father's mother Grandma Kruse and was passed to my mother Frieda Kruse," writes Myrna Nelson of Omaha. "Mom made this recipe often when we were girls. She was a great cook and gave me the recipe when I married in 1955 and started to raise my family. My sister and I now gladly share it with our families."

Combine hamburger, onion, Wheaties, eggs, milk, Worcestershire sauce, celery salt, pepper and sage and then shape in meat loaf pan. Mix topping ingredients in a small bowl and add to loaf. Cover and bake in at 350° for 1 hour.

LOAF

2 lbs hamburger
1 small onion
2 cups Wheaties cereal
2 eggs, beaten
1 cup milk
2 Tbsp Worcestershire sauce
1 tsp celery salt
1/4 tsp pepper
1/4 tsp sage

TOPPING

2 Tbsp brown sugar
2 Tbsp prepared mustard
1 cup ketchup

SERVES 6-8

DOUGH

2	cups warm water
2	packages active dry yeast
1/2	cup sugar
1 ½	tsp salt
1	egg
1/4	cup margarine, melted and cooled
6 ½	cups flour

FILLING

1 ½	lbs hamburger
1/2	cup chopped onion
3	cups shredded cabbage
1/2	cup water
1 ½	tsp salt
1/2	tsp pepper
	Dash of Tabasco (more or less to taste)

SERVES 16

RUNZAS

Lincoln

Former Nebraska First Lady Ruth Raymond Thone of Lincoln writes, "When we moved to Virginia for Charlie's term in Congress back in the '70s, my friend, Aloha Zimmer, of Friend, Neb., sent me this recipe. I didn't know how labor intensive they were to make, but I loved them and used to make and freeze them. Then our girls and their friends would take them when they went to the beaches and on outings. It was something I could give them for a tasty sandwich. The Tabasco is a great variation for spicing up the filling."

Mix water, yeast, sugar, and salt. Stir until dissolved. Add egg and melted margarine. Stir in flour. Put in refrigerator for four hours. Roll dough into an oblong shape and cut into 16 squares.

Brown hamburger and onion. Drain off excess grease. Add cabbage, seasonings and water. Simmer 15-20 minutes. Set aside and cool completely before putting on dough.

Pull four sides up and press edges together. Place on greased cookie sheet and bake at 350° for 20 minutes.

2	lb ground beef
2	Tbsp quick tender salt
1/2	tsp pepper
1	tsp liquid smoke
1/2	tsp onion salt
1/4	tsp garlic salt
1	cup cold water

SERVES 12

LUNCH MEAT SAUSAGE

Elwood

Elinor Lofquist of Elwood got this meat recipe from her mother. "When I make it I think of her."

Mix ingredients with hands. Roll in foil and refrigerate overnight. Bake on cookie sheet with rim at 350° for 1 hour 30 minutes. Remove from foil at once.

Lay out to drain and cool, then wrap in plastic wrap and refrigerate.

CANNED MEAT

Blair and Knox County

"I grew up in western Knox County in the 1930s. Electricity had not yet reached our area so refrigeration was limited to an occasional block of ice for our icebox," writes Eldora Gentzler of Blair.

"Preserving the meat we had butchered was always a challenge. Our favorite was canned beef. After we had freezers, we didn't can as much, but it still remained a favorite. Even today, I can beef as a special treat. I buy either chuck roasts or round roasts. It doesn't need to be choice meat, as the canning process makes it all tender."

HOW TO CAN MEAT

Sterilize jars, lids and rings. Cut roasts into chunks. Pack the chunks into jars. Add 1 tsp canning salt to each quart. Place a small piece of tallow – which you have trimmed from the roast – on the top of the meat. Do not add water. The meat will make its own juice.

Seal and place jars into a kettle which is deep enough to cover the jars with water. Cover the jars in cold water and place over heat. Bring to a boil. Simmer 2 ½ hours, keeping the jars covered with water. Remove the jars from the kettle and check the seals. If you should have a jar that didn't seal, refrigerate or freeze until it is used.

When you open a jar for use, combine enough flour or corn starch with water to make gravy. Add to the meat, heat and serve.

RUNZA CASSEROLE

Omaha

"I've been making this for 47 years," writes Pearl Thunn of Omaha. "I got it from a magazine and altered it a little bit. I made it for my five children and now they're making it for their children. It's so easy to make, cut up and put on a plate."

2	packages crescent rolls
3	cups shredded cabbage
1	lb ground beef
1	can mushroom soup
1	onion, chopped
2-3	cups cheddar cheese
	Salt and pepper to taste

SERVES 6-8

Brown beef and mix with mushroom soup and onion. Cover bottom of 9 x 13-inch pan with one package of rolls. Spread beef mixture on rolls. Spread cabbage layer, then cheddar layer. Top with second package of rolls. Bake at 350° for 30 minutes.

1 lb hamburger
1 can green beans, drained
2 cups potatoes, cut into chunks
1 onion, coarsely chopped
3 carrots, thickly sliced
1 can tomato soup

SERVES 6-8

HAMBURGER GARBAGE CASSEROLE
Atkinson

"I got this recipe from the minister's wife when I was working as a church secretary, probably 50 years ago," writes Marian Bauman of Atkinson. *"She never had a name for it, so we just called it garbage. Now it's a family favorite and my daughter makes it all the time as well."*

Brown hamburger in skillet and drain off grease. Add beans, potatoes, onions and carrots to hamburger. Mix well and spoon into casserole dish. Pour soup on top and bake at 350° for 1 to 1 ½ hours.

Wedding Salisbury Steak

North Bend

"We first had this recipe when my husband's grandmother Anna Arneal in Lenox, Iowa, fixed it for us when we went to visit her and Grandpa JD. I made it over the years for my family and it was always one of their favorites," writes Mary Le Arneal of North Bend.

"When my oldest daughter Corrine was getting married in December 2001, the caterer offered to use one of our recipes. Corrine requested this meat dish. The caterers shaped them into meatballs instead of the usual oval patties, and they were a big hit at the wedding."

Combine saltines, ketchup, onion, parsley, Worcestershire sauce, ground beef, eggs, salt, pepper, marjoram, nutmeg and garlic salt. Mix well. Shape into oval patties or meatballs and place in deep dish, at least 9 x 13-inch. Heat soup, milk, butter/ margarine, sherry and garlic salt. Pour over patties/meatballs. Cover and bake at 350° for 45 minutes. Add mushrooms and pimento during final 10 minutes.

PATTIES

1 ⅔	cups saltines, crushed
1/2	cup ketchup
2	tsp onion, chopped
2	tsp parsley, chopped
1	tsp Worcestershire sauce
2	lbs ground beef
2	eggs
1 ½	tsp salt
1/2	tsp pepper
1/2	tsp marjoram
1/2	tsp nutmeg
	Garlic salt to taste

SAUCE

1	can cream of mushroom soup
1	soup can milk
2	Tbsp butter or margarine
1	tsp sherry
1	4-oz can sliced mushrooms
1	Tbsp chopped pimento

SERVES 6

Gen's Meat and Potato Dish

Columbus

"I acquired this recipe as result of a potluck 40 years ago," writes Helen Fuchs of Columbus. "Neighbors gathered on our driveway to bid farewell to a favorite family who was moving to Omaha. When their casserole appeared, I had to have the recipe, and I have been making it ever since."

Place one half of uncooked ground beef on bottom of a casserole dish and cover with half of potato slices.

Mix soups in bowl and pour half the soup mixture over the potato layer. Repeat layers. Bake uncovered at 350° for one hour, or until potatoes are done. Add French fried onions or crushed potato chips in the final 15 minutes to make a crispy topping.

1 ½	lbs lean ground beef
4-5	medium-size potatoes, thinly sliced
1	can vegetable beef soup
1	can cream of mushroom or beefy mushroom soup French fried onions or crushed potato chips

Serves 6-8

1 ½   lb ground beef
1   15-oz can tomato sauce
1   10-oz can diced tomatoes and green chilies
1   16-oz can small curd cottage cheese
6   6-inch flour tortillas
1   package taco seasoning
4   cups Colby-Jack cheese
1/4   tsp seasoned salt (optional)

SERVES 9-12

TEX MEX LASAGNA
North Platte

"After working 34 years as a hairdresser, I have collected many tried-and-true recipes from my clients, many of them great cooks," writes Monte Brown of North Platte. "This is great for potlucks or family get-togethers because it makes a big batch and makes a pound of hamburger go farther."

Cook beef in a large skillet on medium heat until done. Drain. Add tomato sauce, tomatoes and chilies, taco seasoning and salt. Simmer uncovered for 10 minutes. Spread some meat sauce on bottom of 9 x 13 x 2-inch baking pan.

Top with tortillas and a third of the meat, cottage cheese and then shredded cheese. Repeat layers. Cover and bake at 350° for 30 minutes.

1   lb ground beef
2   lb ground ham
2   eggs
1   cup milk
1   cup crushed graham crackers
1   can tomato soup
1   cup brown sugar
1/4   cup vinegar
1/4   tsp dry mustard

MAKES 12-15 LARGE MEATBALLS

HAM BALLS
Norfolk

"I found this recipe in the newspaper years ago featuring Iowa's Governor Branstad's favorite recipes," writes Jo Schaefer of Norfolk. "I liked it so well we have used it over and over. It has become a family favorite."

In large mixing bowl combine beef, ham, eggs, milk and crackers. Shape meat mixture into 12-15 balls. In small mixing bowl combine tomato soup, sugar, vinegar and mustard; mix well. In a casserole dish or baking pan, place meat balls and cover with sauce. Bake at 375° for 1 hour.

MIRABELLE'S LASAGNA

Fremont

"This recipe was given to me by my daughter's college roommate Mirabelle," writes Martha J. Warehime of Fremont. "Fern and Mirabelle were close in college but each has moved to different states since graduation. We think of Mirabelle every time we make it."

Remove Italian sausage from casings, or cut it into small pieces and add to ground beef.

Brown meats together in large skillet, breaking up meat as you cook. Add spaghetti sauce, garlic powder and parsley flakes to cooked meat. Simmer 15 minutes.

In large stock pan, boil 7 cups water and 2 Tbsp olive oil. Add lasagna noodles, cover pan and turn off heat. Let set for 20 minutes then drain water.

Layer noodles, meat sauce, cream cheese and mozzarella cheese in a deep rectangular dish. Repeat layers until pan is full. A deep dish usually holds three layers. Bake at 350° for 45 minutes.

1	package Italian sausage
1	lb ground beef
1	large jar spaghetti sauce
1/2	tsp garlic powder
1	tsp dried parsley flakes
1	8-oz package lasagna noodles
2	Tbsp olive oil
4	cups mozzarella cheese
1	8-oz package cream cheese, softened

SERVES 6-8

REUBEN CASSEROLE

Springfield, S.D.

"Growing up in South Dakota, we would take our vacations to Nebraska, especially after they opened the bridge at Running Water," writes Patricia Odens of Springfield, S.D. "We made friends in Verdigre and discovered new and wonderful places to visit in Nebraska. This recipe will appeal to the Irish, German, Czech, Nebraskans, South Dakotans… everybody. It isn't one you just make on the spur of the moment, you need to shop and have all your ingredients, because you can't substitute."

Mix soup, onion, milk and mustard in a small bowl until blended. Spread drained sauerkraut in a greased 9 x 13-inch baking dish and top with uncooked noodles. Spoon soup mixture evenly over noodles. Sprinkle with corned beef, then cheese.

Stir together rye bread crumbs and melted butter in a bowl until well-blended then sprinkle over top of cheese. Cover tightly with foil. Bake at 350° for 1 hour or until noodles are tender.

1	12-oz can corned beef, crumbled
1	8-oz package uncooked medium egg noodles
2	16-oz cans sauerkraut, drained
2	cans cream of chicken or mushroom soup
2	cups shredded Swiss cheese
1	cup toasted rye bread crumbs
1/2	cup chopped onion
1 ⅓	cups milk
3	Tbsp prepared mustard
2	Tbsp melted butter

SERVES 6-8

Cowboy Food

At High Plains Homestead

AT THE HIGH PLAINS HOMESTEAD'S DRIFTER COOKSHACK north of Crawford, everyone's a cowboy. They eat like cowboys, at least.

Though his menu is small, owner Mike Kesselring says it's the best cowboy cuisine in the world. And for confused city folks, cowboy cuisine is "nice, big portions of meat-and-potatoes kind of food."

His menu is loaded with steaks, meatloaf, roast and several varieties of potatoes. Cowboy beans are a staple. Sarsaparilla and homemade pie tempt already full customers and leave them smiling.

As for Mike, he likes everything they offer.

"It's what we eat and it's where our family is at," he said.

Mike's folks, Merlin and Roberta Kesselring, created High Plains Homestead in 1998. It's a pioneer village that includes a restaurant, the "Drifter Cookshack." Throughout his years at High Plains Homestead, Mike and his wife Linda have met people from all over Nebraska and the world, giving them a chance to do what the Kesselrings love to do – serve good, home-cooked food to good people.

"We're very fortunate. Everyone that comes to see us are just great people," Mike said.

Mike and Linda also have had ample time to fine-tune Merlin and Roberta's Indian taco recipe, which is a favorite of the family and all the drifters that mosey into the cookshack.

"The Indian Taco has been a cornerstone in the cookshack since its opening day, and it's fair to say it's a definite favorite," he said.

– By Whitney Keyes

Mike and Linda Kesselring, above, and Mike's folks, Merlin and Roberta, have created an Old West village north of Crawford where they serve a mix of cowboy food and family favorites to travelers and tourists.

Indian Taco

Prepare filling by browning and crumbling hamburger in skillet, draining off excess fat. Add taco seasoning and salsa according to taste. Combine water and refried beans, stirring well. Simmer to blend flavors.

Prepare frybread by combining flour, baking powder, salt, powdered milk and sugar in a large bowl. Cut butter into small pieces and cut flour and butter with pastry blender to a fine crumbly mixture. Add warm water and stir with a wooden spoon until just mixed. Use hands to work gently into a ball but do not overwork. The frybread will be more tender and puffy if not kneaded. You may adjust the water slightly to make your dough firm, but supple. Chill dough. The frybread will puff better if cold.

In a heavy skillet, add enough oil to fill to 3/4 inch. Heat cooking oil to 375-400°. Divide dough into 6-8 pieces, or any number, depending on the size you prefer. Roll or pat into a circle about 1/4-inch thick. Slide gently into hot oil, prick several times with fork to keep from turning into a "pillow." Fry on both sides until golden brown. Turn only once. Drain on paper towels. Serve immediately with filling and toppings.

Meat filling

2 ½	lbs hamburger
1-2	packages taco seasoning, depending on taste
1/2	cup salsa
1/2	cup water
1	16-oz can refried beans

Frybread dough

3	cups flour
1	Tbsp baking powder
1	tsp salt
1/4	cup powdered milk
1	Tbsp sugar
1/4	cup butter or margarine
1 ½	cups warm water
	Cooking oil

Toppings

Shredded cheese
Finely cut lettuce
Chopped onions
Tomatoes
Mild green chilies
Sliced black olives
Sour cream
Salsa

Serves 6-8

Apple Streusel Pie

Prepare topping first and chill in refrigerator for easier crumbling. In small bowl, combine melted butter, brown sugar, cinnamon and flour. Mix thoroughly. Chill in refrigerator.

For filling, combine sugar, cinnamon and flour in a small bowl. Toss flour mixture into apples and mix thoroughly. Pour into prepared pie crust.

Crumble topping on top of apples. Bake at 450° for 10 minutes. Cover pie with aluminum foil and turn oven down to 350°. Check pie after 20-30 minutes. Uncover pie for the last 10 minutes. Pie is done when apples are tender and topping is lightly brown and crunchy to the touch.

Filling

3	Tbsp flour
3/4	cup sugar
1	tsp cinnamon
6	cups sliced apples

Topping

1/2	cup butter, melted
1/2	cup brown sugar
1/2	tsp cinnamon
1	cup flour
1	uncooked prepared pie crust

Serves 8

FRIED APPLES, PG. 71   ROASTED ASPARAGUS, PG. 73

Vidalia Onion Pie, pg. 73

Marsha's Dip, pg. 79

Side Dishes

These are more than just recipes; these are memories
of people who have shaped my life.

– Selene Shuster Schulz

5 cups cooked, sliced carrots
1 green pepper, sliced thinly or diced
1 onion, sliced in rings
1 cup sugar
3/4 cup vinegar
1 tsp Worcestershire sauce
1 tsp salt
1 tsp dry mustard
1/2 cup salad oil
1 can undiluted condensed tomato soup
Pepper to taste

SERVES 6-8

MOM'S MARINATED CARROTS

Fremont

"When I take Mom's recipe cards out and see her handwriting I am back in the kitchen peeling carrots or helping her make our favorites," writes Ellen Bonsall of Fremont. "My mother, Ara McCarnan, would have this for Sunday dinner or special occasions. It makes a great salad or as a cold vegetable dish. It's good for summer sides and for those outdoor cookouts and picnics."

Cook, drain and cool carrots. Mix well with green pepper and onion. Mix remaining ingredients well by hand or in blender and pour over vegetables. Marinate 24 hours. Keeps in refrigerator for one week.

CREAMED POTATOES AND PEAS

Dannebrog

"This dish is a must-have at our house as soon as the peas are ready and there are new potatoes in the garden," writes Arlene Obermiller of Dannebrog. "My mother-in-law always made it, but we never really had a recipe for it, so I have come up with this recipe. It is always a hit at potlucks. I hope you enjoy it."

Combine potatoes, peas, onions and salt in large saucepan. Add just enough water to cover vegetables. Cover and cook until potatoes are tender. Drain off half of water. Add evaporated milk and 1 cup milk. Dissolve cornstarch in 1/4 cup milk; add and cook until thickens. Add sugar, butter, salt and pepper.

8-10	new potatoes, quartered
2	cups fresh shelled peas
1	small onion, diced
1/2	tsp salt
1	can evaporated milk, or 1 cup half and half
1 ¼	cups milk
2	tsp cornstarch
2	tsp sugar
5	Tbsp butter
	Salt and pepper to taste

SERVES 6-8

PICKLED BEETS

Wilber

"This recipe came from my grandmother Placek and we have continued to make it throughout the years," write Patricia Spitz of Wilber. "Everyone who has eaten these beets has loved them. It is so simple and yet so good. My son-in-law can never get enough of these beets."

In large pan, combine vinegar, sugar, water, salt and caraway seeds. Bring mixture to boil. Place sliced, peeled beets (and quartered if too large) in boiling water mixture. Reduce heat and simmer 15 minutes. Prepare another large pan with fresh water and bring to boil. Sterilize canning jars by gently dropping jars and lids in fresh boiling water, using tongs. Remove jars with tongs and drain.

Add beets to jars while jars are still hot. Fill jars with sugar/vinegar mixture up to 1/2-inch from top. Wipe excess liquid from rim. Assemble hot lids and rings and tighten. Allow to cool in draft-free place.

3	lbs fresh beets, peeled and tops chopped off, sliced in 1/4-inch rounds
1	cup vinegar
1 ½	cups sugar
1/2	cup water
1/4	tsp salt
	Caraway to taste (approx. 1 tsp per quart)

FILLS 6 QUART JARS

2 package chopped
  spinach
1 large (1 lb, 8 oz)
  carton cottage cheese
6 eggs
1 stick margarine
1 Tbsp flour
1 lb Velveeta cheese
  cut into chunks

SERVES 6-8

SPINACH CASSEROLE

Fremont

"I have always liked spinach, even as a kid, and would eat it out of a can with some vinegar on it," writes Marilyn Gordon of Fremont. *"Not too many people like spinach, so this casserole hides some of that taste. I often serve it when having company as they really don't know exactly what it is and it is a great side dish. My sister-in-law in Seattle wrote last year asking for the recipe; she had lost it and said it was one of their favorites."*

Mix eggs, melted margarine and flour. Add spinach and cheese. Pour in ungreased casserole dish. Bake at 300° for 1 hour 30 minutes.

FRIED APPLES
Brewster

"We have always lived in the Sandhills and I married my husband to come back here," writes June Wescott of Brewster. *"Back in my mother's day they would use anything and everything for meals. I would eat anything but rabbit; they're too cute, even if they wreck your garden! My mother showed me that simple ingredients could be the best, and fried apples were an easy variation of what to do with apples."*

Core and slice apples, but don't peel. Place in a frying pan with butter. Add sugar depending on how tart the apples are. Cover and fry slowly, turning apples frequently.

4	apples
2-3	Tbsp butter
1/2	cup sugar

SERVES 4-6

DADDY'S DUMPLINGS
Cozad

"Dad has always been the chief cook in our family," writes Jo Ann Parker of Cozad. *"No matter what the menu was, my sister and I begged for his potato dumplings. No one could make them as well as Dad could, and you couldn't have the dumplings without sauerkraut. Not everybody in the family agrees to this combination, but for the rest of us it was an absolute must."*

Grind raw potatoes. Drain excess water with a paper towel. Grind cooked potatoes and mix with raw potatoes in a large mixing bowl. Add egg to potatoes and mix well. Add enough flour to hold mixture together and mix well.

Fill large kettle with water and bring to boil. Wet hands and shape potato mixture into golf ball size balls. Place balls into boiling water. When dumplings float to the top they are done. Serve with sauerkraut or butter. Salt and pepper to taste.

4-5	raw potatoes
3-4	cooked potatoes
1	egg
	Flour
	Salt and pepper

MAKES 8 DUMPLINGS

1   can pork and beans
1   can green beans,
     drained
1   can lima beans
1   can butter beans
1   can garbanzo beans
1   can red kidney beans
1   can northern beans
1   can yellow wax beans
1   can chili beans with
     sauce
1   lb bacon, cooked and
     crumbled
1 ½   cups ketchup
5   Tbsp Worcestershire
     sauce
1 ½   cups brown sugar
1/2   cup tarragon vinegar
3   tsp dry mustard

SERVES 12

SHIELD BEANS
Norfolk

Eleanor McIntosh of Norfolk sends this recipe:

Drain all beans except pork and beans and chili beans. Combine ingredients and place in 9 x 13-inch greased baking pan. Bake at 350° for 1 hour.

14   corn cobs
1   package Sure-Jell
3   cups sugar
3-4   drops red food
     coloring

MAKES 2 PINTS

CORNCOB JELLY
Kenesaw

"My mother-in-law made lots of batches of this and put it in small baby food jars," writes Virginia Short of Kenesaw. "She had everybody saving her baby jars. Then when they went to the Agriculture Services Convention she would set one at each plate. She put a little ribbon tie around the lid and glued a decoration to it. She did this for several years and people always looked forward to getting her jelly."

Wash cobs to remove chaff. In a large pan, cover cobs with water. Boil gently for 30 minutes. The cobs will absorb water, so be sure to use plenty. Strain 3 cups of the red corn liquor into a pan. Add the Sure-Jell and let this come to a hard boil. Add sugar. Bring to a fast boil and boil hard for 1 minute. Add food coloring. Set aside and skim.

ROASTED ASPARAGUS
Oregon City, Ore.

"I had this dish at a French restaurant in San Francisco in 1963, writes Martin Shubin of Oregon City, Ore. "The restaurant was located at the old Barbary Coast section of the city. This was my first introduction to fine dining in the big city after leaving the farm."

Cut bottoms off asparagus at an angle. Sprinkle salt and pepper on asparagus before cooking. Wrap asparagus with prosciutto. Wipe cookie sheet with olive oil and place wrapped asparagus on cookie sheet. Sprinkle with olive oil or truffle olive oil. Roast in a preheated oven at 375° for 20 minutes or until done.

2   bunches asparagus
1/3 cup olive oil or truffle olive oil
2   packages prosciutto (Italian ham)
    Salt and pepper to taste

SERVES 4-6

VIDALIA ONION PIE
Syracuse

"My neighbor gave this recipe to me many years ago," writes Karen Johnson of Syracuse. "The family enjoys it, it is simple to make and when the Vidalia onions are in season we look forward to many meals of our onion pie."

Mix cracker crumbs with 1/4 cup melted butter or margarine. Press crumbs into an 8-inch pie plate. Sauté onions in 2 tsp butter until translucent, not brown. Spoon onions onto cracker crust. Beat eggs, milk, salt and pepper. Pour over onions. Sprinkle with cheese and dot with paprika. Bake at 350° for 30 minutes or until knife comes out clean.

1   cup crushed Ritz crackers
1/4 cup melted butter or margarine
2   cups Vidalia onions, sliced thin
2   tsp butter or margarine
2   eggs
3/4 cup milk
3/4 tsp salt
1/4 cup grated cheddar cheese
    Dash pepper
    Paprika

SERVES 8

3 cucumbers, thinly
   sliced
3 tsp salt
2-3 cups water
1 cup sour cream
1/2 cup vinegar
1/2 cup sugar

SERVES 6 OR MORE

GRANDMOTHER'S SOUR CREAM 'N CUCUMBERS

Austin, Minn.

"Even though my grandparents had 10 children and were not wealthy people, they took in others who were in need," writes Selene Shuster Schulz of Austin, Minn. "My grandparents came from Kearney and my mother grew up in Denman. On Sundays, the married children and their families would come to the family farm to eat together.

"That tradition carried on to the next generation and the next generation. No matter how much or little money we had in our home while growing up, food was meant to be shared with those you love. I was amazed what a good meal my mother and aunts could make out of nothing with little or no notice."

Dissolve salt in water and pour over cucumbers. Let stand 30 minutes. Drain thoroughly. Combine remaining ingredients. Add to cucumbers and mix well. Let stand at least 3 minutes. May be chilled before serving.

ZUCCHINI PATTIES
Minden

"We run Grace Elizabeth's Bed and Breakfast in Minden," writes Sonya Nelsen of Minden. "Most of our recipes we use come from our dear Grace Elizabeth's recipe box and are enjoyed by family, friends and guests."

Combine biscuit mix, cheese, salt, eggs, zucchini and onion; blend well. Melt butter in large skillet and spoon heaping tablespoons of mixture into skillet. Fry 3 minutes per side, or until golden brown. Place browned patties on paper towel. Add more butter to skillet for additional batches. You can dip these in marinara sauce for added flavor.

1	cup Bisquick or other baking mix
1/2	cup shredded mozzarella or cheddar cheese
1/8	tsp salt
2	eggs, beaten
2	cups shredded zucchini
2	tsp chopped onion (optional)
1	tsp butter

SERVES 4-6

SQUASH CASSEROLE
Big Springs

Juanita Zoucha of Big Springs writes that this recipe is "a very favorite at our house, especially for the winter holidays."

Combine ingredients and bake in a greased casserole at 350° for 30 minutes.

1	quart cooked and mashed squash (butternut or Hubbard are good)
1/2	cup sour cream
1	Tbsp dried or minced onion
1	Tbsp butter
	Salt and pepper to taste

SERVES 6-8

Golden Mac and Cheese

Burr

"I found this recipe years ago and adapted it to suit our family," writes Amy Oswalt of Burr. *"Every time I have a family gathering I have to make this. I get raves for it every time! I even converted my seven-year-old niece, who normally eats the blue-boxed mac and cheese, to home-baked mac and cheese."*

1	8-oz package elbow macaroni
2	cups milk
1/4	cup flour
1	tsp onion salt
2	10 oz blocks sharp cheddar cheese
1	cup soft breadcrumbs
1/4	cup butter or margarine, melted

Serves 8

Cook macaroni according to package directions, drain well and set aside. Place milk, flour and onion salt in a quart jar, cover tightly and shake vigorously for 1 minute. Shred cheese and stir together 3 ½ cups with the flour mixture and macaroni

Pour macaroni into a lightly greased 9 x 13-inch pan. Sprinkle evenly with rest of cheese and then breadcrumbs. Drizzle evenly with butter. Bake at 350° for 45 minutes or until golden brown.

POTATO PUFFS
North Platte

"There were nine children in our family," writes Lenora Gocke of North Platte. "As the eldest, I was mother's helper in the kitchen. Whenever we had leftover mashed potatoes from the noon meal, we made these potato puffs."

Sift flour with black and white pepper and salt. Combine beaten eggs with potatoes and flour mixture. Drop by tablespoonfuls into hot grease and fry until golden brown.

1/2	cup flour
1 ½	tsp black pepper
1/4	tsp salt
2	eggs, well beaten
1	cup mashed potatoes
	Dash of white pepper

SERVES 4-6

BREAD & BUTTER PICKLES
Atascadero, Calif.

"I was raised in the Great Depression of the 1930s and would not have survived without mother's diligence in canning hundreds of quarts of fruits, vegetables, meats and jam," writes Sylvia Clawson English of Atascadero, Calif. "As an ex-Nebraskan, I still love Nebraska and know plenty of people who still can their food, just not like they used to."

Wash cucumbers. Layer sliced cucumbers and onions in a bowl. Sprinkle each layer with salt. Let stand 3 hours. Drain and rinse off salt water. In a large stock pot, combine water, vinegar, sugar, celery seeds, mustard seeds and salt.

Bring to boil and cook until sugar is dissolved. Continue to boil for another 3 minutes. Add cucumbers and onions and bring to boil. Remove from heat. Place cucumber and onions in hot sterilized jars and seal.

8	medium cucumbers, thinly sliced
6	white onions, sliced
3/4	cup salt
2	cups water
1	qt white vinegar
4	cups granulated sugar
2	Tbsp celery seeds
2	Tbsp mustard seeds

MAKES 8 QUARTS

1/2   cup sugar
1/2   cup hot water
 1   bottle Cuthills
     Vineyards
     La Crosse
1/2   cup Cactus Juice
     (Dekuyper
     Margarita Liquor)
 2   limes cut into
     chunks
 1   orange cut into
     chunks
 1   lemon cut into
     chunks
 1   cup tonic water

MAKES 1/2 GALLON

MARGARITA SANGRIA
Pierce

"We were having a wedding reception at the winery when I came up with this,"
writes Holly Swanson of Cuthills Vineyards. "I was thinking of other drinks to serve
while shopping at the grocery store, and this just came to mind. We had just finished
bottling the La Crosse and decided to use it for the sangria, but any of the whites will
work fine."

Place sugar in measuring cup and add hot water. Stir until dissolved. Add all other
ingredients together in a pitcher, squeezing the fruit and adding sugar mixture.
Cover and refrigerate 1-2 hours before serving.

MARSHA'S DIP
South Sioux City

"We lost Marsha to cancer some years ago," writes Dona Dean Lovell of South Sioux City. "She was a treasure to be sure, very talented and special. I found this recipe in her handwriting as we were preparing a recipe shower for a new bride-to-be in our church. Marsha's dip base is easy to make spicy or mild. Any toppings will do, meat or not, it is sure to be a winner. Be sure you have enough chips!"

In small bowl mix cream cheese and milk, stir until smooth. On a platter spread cream cheese. Cover with taco sauce. Layer the toppings of your choice over taco sauce and cream cheese. Chill at least one hour. Serve with chips or crackers.

1	package cream cheese, softened
2	Tbsp milk
1	12-oz jar taco sauce
	Tomatoes, diced
	Green peppers, diced
	Black olives, sliced
	Lettuce, shredded
	Cheddar cheese, shredded
	Chips or crackers

SERVES 6

CORN RELISH
Kent, Wash.

"I remember helping Mother make this recipe," writes Geraldine Miles of Kent, Wash. "Born and raised, in Lincoln I remember those days of picking the corn in our garden and canning lots of it. Afterward, the kitchen would smell so good. With family is still in Nebraska I try to get out to visit as often as I can."

Cut corn from cob. Add other ingredients and put into a deep pan. Place in cold oven. Cook at 400° for 2 hours to 2 hours 30 minutes. Stir often to prevent sticking to the pan. Pour into jars and seal.

12	ears sweet corn
12	onions, chopped
3	green peppers, chopped
4	cups chopped cabbage
4	cups vinegar
2	cups sugar
1	Tbsp ground mustard
1	Tbsp celery seed
1/4	tsp tumeric
2	tsp salt

SERVES 12-16

2 10-oz package frozen peas
1 cup chopped onion
1 cup chopped water chestnuts
1 cup chopped celery
1 small jar chopped pimiento, drained
1 can cream of mushroom soup
1 cup bread crumbs, buttered if desired

Serves 6-8

Holiday Peas

Fremont

"I'm a transplant to Nebraska from Ohio over 30 years ago," writes Ellen Bonsall of Fremont. "This state has become home to me and I've learned a lot from some wonderful Nebraska cooks. I got this recipe from my first Nebraska cookbook when we first moved here and I make this every Christmas without fail."

Cook peas according to directions. Drain most of water. Mix ingredients and place in a greased 9 x 13-inch casserole. Top with bread crumbs. Bake at 350° for 30 minutes until bubbly.

SCALLOPED TOMATOES

Ralston

"This 1930s recipe comes from my mother Maxine Kessinger," writes Kayleen Kessinger Elson of Ralston. "In those days everything was used, nothing was ever thrown away. This is great for a potluck, buffet or a family dinner. The olives and grated cheese were added years later, but I think it is a nice addition."

Melt 2 Tbsp butter in small pan and stir in bread crumbs until lightly browned. Set aside for topping. Melt 2 Tbsp butter in large skillet and stir in onion. Cook until onions are limp. Add tomatoes, tapioca and seasonings. Cook 5 minutes, stirring constantly.

Grease a 3-quart casserole dish. Sprinkle half of the toasted crumbs on bottom of casserole dish. Add tomato mixture, grated cheese and olives. Top with remaining crumbs. Bake at 350° for 40 minutes.

2	Tbsp minced onion
3	cups canned tomatoes
5	Tbsp minute tapioca
1	Tbsp sugar
1/2	tsp paprika
1	cup grated cheddar cheese
3/4	cup sliced stuffed olives
1	cup dry bread crumbs
4	Tbsp melted butter
	Salt and pepper to taste

SERVES 6

GREEN TOMATO PARMESAN

Atkinson

"I learned to garden and cook from my mother," writes Claudeen Penry from Atkinson. "We have always had a garden and at the end of the season we would use the unripe green tomatoes, not wanting to waste anything, by frying them. I grow a variety of tomatoes and have now added Roma tomatoes in my patch, but I have not tried growing the true green tomato. Any variety of green tomato will fry up nicely."

Lightly sprinkle tomatoes with salt and drain on paper towels for 30 minutes. Combine cornmeal, cheese, flour, garlic salt, oregano and pepper in shallow plate. Dip each tomato slice into egg and cornmeal mixture.

In skillet, heat oil over medium high heat. Fry tomatoes a few at a time for 2 minutes per side, or until golden. Drain and serve immediately.

3	medium green tomatoes, sliced 1/4-inch thick
1/4	cup cornmeal
1/4	cup grated parmesan cheese
2	Tbsp flour
3/4	tsp garlic salt
1/2	tsp dried oregano
1/8	tsp pepper
1	egg, beaten
1/4	cup vegetable oil
	Salt

SERVES 2-4

Henderson Mennonites

And their verenike, apple prietska and zwieback

I F YOU REALLY ARE WHAT YOU EAT, then the Henderson Mennonites are a testimony to frugality – the waste not, want not, stretch-a-meal-to-feed-a-house-full variety. And flavor – the kind that sticks to your ribs, sustains you through an afternoon of hard work and makes leftovers something to anticipate.

But the laughter and chatter that greets you in Mary Ellen Pankratz' kitchen belie centuries of religious persecution faced by Mennonites whose commitment to faith often found them homeless. After fleeing Russia, their sad path of displacement through Europe brought them by the hundreds to "The Great American Dessert" where they settled in Henderson and the surrounding area as early as 1874.

Large trunks accompanied the immigrants, packed conservatively with just the necessities. Nonetheless, folded in women's undergarments were flower bulbs and saplings of fruit trees, because life without colorful gardens and apple prieska was unthinkable. And, of course, everyone had found some space for the thousands of zwieback roasted prior to leaving Russia which nourished them, body and soul, across the Atlantic Ocean.

A community comprised of people familiar with struggle is a community which knows

Above, from left, Mary Ellen Pankratz, Nadine Peters and JoAnne Buller of Henderson. The traditional meal they've all contributed to consists of (front row, from left) apple prieska, homemade noodles in gravy; (center) a platter of ham with both boiled and fried verenike, and (back row) two baskets of zwieback. Next page, Mary Ellen Pankratz and her famous apple prieska. Scott Friesen is trying to snag a treat (so typical!)

Apple Prieska

Mix ingredients for the pie crust. Roll out until thin and cut into 4-5 inch squares.

Slice apples into bite-size pieces and mix with sugar and clear gel.

Top each square with 1/2 cup apple filling. Bring up four corners and pinch. Bake at 400° for 20-30 minutes. Remove immediately to cool on baking rack.

Crust

4 ½	cup flour
1/2	tsp baking powder
1 ½	cup lard or shortening
2	tsp salt
1	cup cold water
1	Tbsp vinegar

Filling

8	cups sliced apples
2	cups sugar
2	Tbsp clear gel

Makes 30

how to work together. The noodles JoAnne Buller uses in her ham and noodle recipe are the very same used by the women's auxiliary for the fall soup feed to benefit the hospital. In the ample kitchen at the Bethesda Mennonite Church the number of noodles made in advance is best counted by the 90 dozen eggs cracked one-handed. But even at home, JoAnne makes more noodles than she needs. "When I was young we didn't have freezers," she said. "Even now I dry them and put them in Tupperware."

Likewise, when Mary Ellen isn't steaming up the kitchen with the verenike, apple prietska and zwieback – which she supplies to Henderson Food Mart – she's finding other ways to reach her community with the food they love. In March she assists with the school's smorgasbord, a fundraiser for the band program. "They still make their own cottage cheese," she said. "It's so much better – made from cream left to warm on the back of the stove until it curdles."

Food made from whatever the farm produces, which has the capability to feed, nourish and support an entire community, is worthy of celebration. Or, at the very least, company for Sunday dinner.

– By Kristen Friesen

2 cups milk
(warmed
to 108°)
1 cup water
3 Tbsp yeast
1/3 cup sugar
* Combine first
four ingredients
until yeast begins
to bubble

TO MIXTURE
ADD:
1 Tbsp salt
1 cup melted
margarine
(not too hot)
8 cups flour

MAKES 3 DOZEN

ZWIEBACK
(pronounced zwee-bock or tway-bock) – literally "two-bakes"

Mix dough in mixer for 5-10 minutes. Place in oiled bowl until doubled. Punch down and allow dough to rise until doubled in bulk again. Form into walnut sized balls and stack one on top of another (2 high). Let those rise until doubled in size. Bake at 400° for 10-12 minutes.

CREAMED GRAVY

2 cups cream (sour,
sweet or both)
2/3 cup ham broth or
drippings
1 Tbsp flour
Salt and pepper to
taste

SERVES 6

HAM AND NOODLES WITH CREAMED GRAVY

Make dough for noodles using these proportions:

For each egg used add 1 Tbsp water, 1/8-1/4 tsp salt and enough flour to make stiff, roll-able dough. Roll dough until very thin. Cut into strips 1 ½-2 inches wide. Place one strip on top of another using plenty of flour between each layer (to prevent sticking) until stack is 1-inch high. Cut across ends, slicing off the noodles in desired widths. Noodles may be dried like commercial noodles for later use, or cooked immediately.

To cook: place slowly into boiling water until dough is done and tender. Drain and pour creamed gravy over them.

Mix ingredients for creamed gravy in saucepan. Heat slowly and thicken with corn starch (hickory smoked ham base adds additional flavor).

Serve alongside fried or otherwise prepared ham. Cubed ham may also be combined with the noodles for a pasta main dish variation.

VERENIKE
(pronounced "vuh-ren-ih-kuh")

Combine ingredients for dough in mixer and beat 5-10 minutes with a dough hook. Let rest while you make cottage cheese filling.

Place ingredients for cottage cheese filling in mixer and beat with a paddle until it forms together.

On lightly floured board, roll out dough until quite thin. Cut out circles using a 1-lb coffee can. Scoop one #40 dipper of cottage cheese mixture onto each circle of dough. Fold in half and seal edges. Verenike can be frozen or immediately cooked, pan fried or deep fat fried.

To cook: boil in water, stir gently until they're finished and float to the top.

Note: Shirley Goertzen of Lincoln makes verenike "casserole style" by alternating layers of creamed gravy (see recipe opposite page), cooked lasagna noodles and the dry curd cottage cheese mixture. Cubed ham can be added to the gravy for a one-dish meal. Bake 325° for 30-40 minutes.

DOUGH
2	eggs
1/2	cup cream
1/2	cup milk
1	tsp salt
3-3 ¼	cup flour (enough to make stiff dough)

FILLING
4	cup dry curd cottage cheese
3	eggs
1	tsp salt
1	tsp pepper

MAKES 25-30

CHICAGO PIE, PG. 115

PINKY THAYER'S TIN ROOF SUNDAE, PG. 101

COLA CAKE, PG. 111

JOANN'S CAKE, PG. 106

Desserts

Electricity came to our farm in Madison County the
fall of 1940. Although I was only four years old, I
vividly remember the first purchases: an iron, washing
machine and refrigerator. My mother was delighted
with all three of these but it was the refrigerator
that we kids thought was magical.

– Geri Weiland Loecker

2 cups brown sugar
4 eggs
1 Tbsp cold water
2 cups flour
1/4 tsp salt
2 cups pecans
2 cups gum drops, sliced
1/2 tsp cinnamon

Makes 24 bars

Gum Drop Bars

Oconomowoc, Wisc.

"This is one of the few recipes my grandmother actually wrote down," writes Karen Schoenike of Oconomowoc, Wisc. "I grew up in Bushnell and my mom, Minnie Olive Smith, youngest of ten children, lives in Chadron. In Mom's day, gum drops came in only one size: giant. As a small kid, my mom remembers 'helping' by cutting the gum drops into small pieces."

Whisk eggs very lightly; add cold water and brown sugar, mixing well. Sift together flour, cinnamon and salt. Put a spoonful of the flour mixture into the pecans and gum drops (don't use licorice). Stir well and sift off the excess flour mix. Add all the flour to the egg mixture and finally add the nuts and gum drops. Spread in a greased cookie sheet 3/8-inch thick.

Bake at 325° for 30 minutes, or until brown. Cool slightly, then remove from pan and cut into bars. Frost each bar and decorate with gum drops.

FRUIT COBBLER
Wakefield

"We have 22 acres of gardens, and most of my produce usually comes from my garden," writes Karen Sherer of Wakefield. "We now have grandkids helping us with the garden, and they love to sell the fruits and veggies at the farmer's markets. All my recipes have been handed down from my family by trading recipes at the family reunions."

Pour fruit into an 8 x 8-inch pan. In mixing bowl, cream together 3/4 cup sugar and butter. Add milk, flour, salt and baking powder. Pour over fruit layer. In separate mixing bowl, combine 1 cup sugar, corn starch and salt. Sprinkle this over second layer. Pour boiling water over all and bake at 375° for 1 hour.

FIRST LAYER
3-4 cups rhubarb or apples

SECOND LAYER
3/4 cup sugar
3 Tbsp butter
1/3 cup milk
1 cup flour
1/4 tsp salt
1 tsp baking powder

THIRD LAYER
1 cup sugar
1 Tbsp corn starch
1/4 tsp salt
1 cup boiling water

SERVES 8

FUDGE PUDDLES
Ravenna

"These are really easy to make and so handy to have because of their bite-size servings," said Nedra Wilkinson of Ravenna. "I have 15 grandkids, ages 6 to 25, and they love them. My kids don't really make them, so they're a 'Grandma's-only' treat."

Beat together margarine or butter, peanut butter and sugars. Add eggs and vanilla. Stir together flour, soda and salt. Stir flour mixture into creamed mixture. Chill at least one hour. Shape into 48 balls, 1 inch in diameter and bake in mini muffin pans at 325° for 14-16 minutes. Remove from oven and immediately make "wells" with melon baller. Cool in pan 5 minutes and remove.

For the filling, melt chips in a double boiler over water. Stir in milk and vanilla. Fill each shell using a pastry bag to pipe in filling. Sprinkle with nuts.

DOUGH
1/2 cup margarine or butter
1/2 cup creamy peanut butter
1/2 cup sugar
1/2 cup light brown sugar
1 egg
1/2 tsp vanilla
1 ¼ cup flour
3/4 tsp baking soda
1/2 tsp salt

FILLING
1 cup milk chocolate chips
1 cup semi-sweet chocolate chips
1 can sweetened condensed milk
1 tsp vanilla

MAKES 4 DOZEN

DOUGH

4	cups all purpose flour
1/4	cup unsweetened cocoa powder
1	tsp salt
2	cups powdered sugar
2	cups softened butter
4	tsp vanilla

FILLING

2/3	cup evaporated milk
2/3	cup granulated sugar
2	egg yolks, beaten
1/3	cup butter
1	tsp vanilla
3/4	cup chopped pecans
1 ¼	cup shredded coconut

TOPPING

1/2	cup semisweet chocolate chips
2	Tbsp water
2	Tbsp butter
1/2	cup powdered sugar

MAKES 3 DOZEN

GERMAN CHOCOLATE COOKIES
Howells

"These are excellent and worth the work," writes Michelle Kumke of Howells. "Use fresh ingredients to get the best results. I get raves every time I make them and am constantly being asked to make more!"

In medium bowl, sift together flour, cocoa and salt. Set aside. Use an electric mixer to cream powdered sugar, butter and vanilla in a large mixing bowl. Blend flour mixture into butter mixture. Dough will be stiff. Use your hands to knead ingredients together. Using about 2 Tbsp at a time, form dough into balls.

Place balls on ungreased cookie sheet and make indentation in center of each ball with finger. Bake at 350° for 12-14 minutes, or until cookies are slightly browned. Remove from cookie sheet immediately and cool on wire racks.

To make filling, combine milk, sugar, egg yolks, butter and vanilla in a saucepan. Cook over a medium heat, stirring constantly. Mixture will become slightly thick and gold in color in 5-8 minutes. Remove from heat and allow to thicken as it cools. Add pecans and coconut, stirring well. Let cool 15-20 minutes. Drop a small amount of filling in the indentation of each cookie. Let cool.

To make topping, combine chocolate chips, water and butter in a saucepan over low heat. Stir constantly until smooth. Add sugar and beat until smooth. Drizzle over cookies.

Cinnamon Pudding Cake

Comstock

"This coffee cake recipe was known in our family as 'cinnamon pudding' that my mother made," writes Twila Lenstrom of Comstock. *"We called it pudding because Mother did. She would serve it with country whipped cream that came from the milk separator, separating the milk from the cream. Now that's fresh!"*

Combine brown sugar, 1 Tbsp butter and water in small pan to make syrup. Bring to boil and pour into greased 9-inch square pan. In a small pan, warm milk and 2 Tbsp melted butter. In medium mixing bowl, combine flour, sugar, baking powder and cinnamon. Add warm milk and butter and mix with dry ingredients. Pour over the syrup mixture and spread as evenly as possible without mixing up the syrup. Top with nuts. Bake at 350° for 40-45 minutes. Serve with whipped cream.

1	cup brown sugar
3	Tbsp butter
2	cups flour
1	cup sugar
2	tsp baking powder
2	tsp cinnamon
1	cup milk
1/2	cup pecans or walnuts, halved or chopped
3/4	cup water
	Whipped cream for serving

SERVES 9-12

German Chocolate Cake

Pierce

"This is my husband's favorite," writes Sandy Korth of Pierce. *"I bake two of these cakes around his birthday so he has one at home and one to share at his workplace; otherwise, he gets a lot of grief when they see him eating a piece for his lunch."*

Grease 3 round layer pans (8-inch or 9-inch) or two square 8 x 8-inch or 9 x 9-inch pans. Line bottom of pans with waxed paper or spray with Baker's Joy. In small bowl, pour boiling water over chocolate, stirring until melted. Set aside to cool.

In a large mixing bowl, cream butter and sugar until light and fluffy. Add egg yolks, one at a time, beating after each addition. On low speed, blend in chocolate and vanilla. Mix in flour, soda and salt alternately with buttermilk, beating after each addition until batter is smooth. Fold in egg whites. Divide batter among pans.

Bake layers at 350° until the top springs back when touched lightly. The times vary as follows:

8-inch round layers: 35-40 minutes	8-inch square layers: 45-50 minutes
9-inch round layers: 30-35 minutes	9-inch square layers: 40-45 minutes

Cool 15 minutes before removing from pans. Fill layers and frost top of cake with coconut-pecan frosting. To make the frosting, combine evaporated milk, sugar, egg yolks, butter and vanilla in small saucepan. Cook and stir over medium heat until thick, 12-15 minutes. Stir in coconut and pecans. Beat until thick enough to spread.

CAKE

1	4-oz bar sweet cooking chocolate
1	cup butter or margarine, softened
2	cups sugar
4	egg yolks
1	tsp vanilla
2 ½	cups cake flour
1	tsp soda
1/2	tsp salt
1	cup buttermilk
4	egg whites, stiffly beaten
1/2	cup boiling water

FROSTING

1	cup evaporated milk
1	cup sugar
3	egg yolks
1/2	cup butter or margarine
1	tsp vanilla
1 ½	cup flaked coconut
1	cup chopped pecans

SERVES 10-12

5   eggs, separated
1   tsp vanilla
4   Tbsp (level) cocoa
1   Tbsp (rounded) flour
1   cup powdered sugar
1 ½ cups heavy whipping
    cream
3-6 Tbsp granulated
    sugar, more or less
    to sweeten to taste
1   tsp vanilla
    Dash of salt

SERVES 10-12

CHOCOLATE CAKE ROLL

Talmage

"This is a recipe my mother, Luella (Kohrs) Adams, made when she wanted a special dessert," writes Mary Teten of Talmage. *"It sounds difficult, but is really quick and easy. I make it often for my family for their birthdays rather than a cake."*

In a small mixing bowl, beat egg whites until very stiff. In large mixing bowl, beat egg yolks with vanilla. On waxed paper, sift cocoa, flour, sugar and salt and add to egg yolks. Mix well. Fold egg whites into batter.

Line a large (10 x 15-inch) baking pan with parchment paper. Spread a very thin layer over the parchment paper and bake 325° for 15-20 minutes.

When the cake is done, wring out two flour sack dish towels (not terry cloth) from hot water and lay one flat on the counter. Turn out the cake onto one dish towel. Remove parchment paper. Place other dish towel on top of cake. Using the damp towels, roll up the cake gently, but not too tight. This just "forms" the cake into a roll. Do not let cake cool completely.

Whip heavy cream into stiff peaks. Add sugar a little at a time to the stiff cream. Add vanilla.

Before the cake is cool, unroll and remove top towel. Spread whipped cream on cake. Re-roll cake using bottom towel to roll. Whipped cream is now between rolls. Use bottom towel to transfer cake to platter. Remove towel. Refrigerate until ready to serve. Use chocolate syrup, powdered sugar or other toppings to decorate.

APRICOT BARS

Merna

Shirley Gottula sends this favorite dessert recipe from Merna:

"This was my mom's bar recipe. She would make them and it wouldn't take long until they were gone. Today I make them for my kids and co-workers, and they're everybody's favorite."

In a large bowl, beat butter and sugar. Add egg and mix well. In a separate bowl, combine flour and baking powder. Gradually add to butter mixture. Add coconut, walnuts and vanilla. Mix thoroughly.

   Press two-thirds of dough into a greased 9 x 13-inch pan. Spread with preserves; crumble remaining dough over preserves. Bake at 350° for 30-35 minutes.

3/4	cup margarine
1	cup sugar
1	egg
2	cups flour
1/4	tsp baking powder
1/2	cup chopped walnuts
1/2	tsp vanilla extract
1	jar apricot preserves
1 ⅓	cup shredded coconut

SERVES 12

STREUSEL BUTTERMILK CAKE

Norfolk

"I found this recipe a long time ago," writes Ruth Haller of Norfolk. "We use it for all kinds of occasions. The family especially likes chocolate frosting on it, and now we use it for birthday cake."

Prepare cake by creaming butter and sugar together in large mixing bowl. Add eggs, one at a time, beating after each one. Add flour, baking powder, baking soda, and salt, mixing well. Add buttermilk and vanilla. Set aside.

   Make crumb topping by mixing cracker crumbs, brown sugar, melted butter and chopped nuts together in medium mixing bowl. Set aside.

   Grease and flour a 9 x 13-inch pan and pour in half of cake mixture. Sprinkle half of crumb topping over first layer. Pour remaining cake mixture over crumb topping then top with remaining cracker crumbs. Bake at 350° for 40-45 minutes or until toothpick comes out clean.

   Combine powdered sugar and milk in small bowl to make glaze mixture. Drizzle over cooled cake.

CAKE
1	cup butter
2	cups sugar
4	eggs
3	cups sifted flour
1/2	tsp baking powder
1/4	tsp baking soda
1/4	tsp salt
1	cup buttermilk
2	tsp vanilla

CRUMB TOPPING
2	cups graham cracker crumbs (20 crackers)
3/4	cup brown sugar
3/4	cup butter, melted
3/4	cup chopped nuts

GLAZE
1 ½	cup powdered sugar
2-3	Tbsp milk

SERVES 12-16

3/4 cup butter or margarine
1/3 cup brown sugar
1 ¼ cup flour
2 packages unflavored gelatin
1/2 cup cold water
2 cups white sugar
1/4 cup water
1/4 cup maraschino cherry juice
1/2 cup chopped, drained maraschino cherries
1/2 cup chopped nuts (optional)
   Flaked coconut

MAKES 3-4 DOZEN

CHERRY MARSHMALLOWS
York

"This recipe came from my mother in law," writes Ann Eddy of York. *"It is a good recipe for those with allergies because it has no eggs. I have made this with pineapple instead of cherries and it is just as good."*

Blend butter, brown sugar and flour and pat into a 13 x 9-inch pan. Bake at 325° for 20 minutes. In a large mixer bowl, soak unflavored gelatin with 1/2 cup cold water. Stir to dissolve. While this is soaking, boil together sugar, 1/4 cup water, and cherry juice for 2 minutes. Pour over the softened gelatin and beat at high speed for a FULL 10 minutes.

   Add the chopped cherries and nuts. Pour over crust and chill 30 minutes. Cut into squares and roll in flaked coconut. May substitute pineapple juice and crushed pineapple for the cherry juice and cherries.

2 cups milk, scalded
2 cups dry bread broken into small pieces
2 eggs
1/3 cup sugar
1/4 tsp salt
1/2 tsp cinnamon
1 cup raisins
1/2 tsp vanilla
   Nutmeg

SERVES 6

BREAD PUDDING
Culbertson

"My grandmother, born in 1900, made this often," writes Liana Rich of Culbertson. *"She used to make delicious bread several times a week but never used a recipe. I wished I had asked her years ago to write down her recipes but in those days they knew everything from memory."*

In mixing bowl, pour scalded milk over bread. Let stand until soft. In separate mixing bowl, combine eggs, sugar, salt, cinnamon, raisins and vanilla. Add to bread mixture and mix well. Pour into a greased 8 x 8-inch baking dish and sprinkle with nutmeg. Bake at 325° for 1 hour 15 minutes. Tip: To scald milk, cook milk in a sauce pan on high heat, but do not allow it to boil.

CHERRY MASH
Encino, Calif.

"Cherry mash candy has brightened our seasonal cookie platters as long as I can remember," writes Michelle

Warren of Encino, Calif. *"We are all farm gals as far back as my great grandmother, and we have prepared it for both Thanksgiving and Christmas. It looks like, but tastes better than the famous Twin Bing candy bars from Sioux City. We didn't realize how regional this candy was until we moved to the West Coast. We shopped and searched, but no store carried cherry chips. I now order cherry chips online and it is worth the price to have my Nebraskan homemade holiday morsel of heaven."*

In a medium saucepan, melt the sugar, evaporated milk, marshmallows, butter and dash of salt. Once melted, boil for 6 minutes. Add cherry chips, vanilla and half of chopped Spanish peanuts. Stir well. Pour into a buttered 9 x 13-inch pan. Cool.

In separate medium saucepan, combine chocolate chips, peanut butter and remaining Spanish peanuts. Stir on low heat until melted. Spread melted chocolate layer on top of firm chilled cherry layer. Cut into 1-inch squares.

2	cups granulated sugar
2/3	cup evaporated milk
12	jumbo marshmallows
1/2	cup butter
10	oz cherry chips
1	lb chopped Spanish peanuts, skins on
1	tsp vanilla
12	oz semi sweet chocolate chips
3/4	cup peanut butter
	Dash of salt

MAKES 36 SQUARES

"CHERRY CRAB" COFFEE CAKE
Norfolk

"I don't remember for sure where I got his recipe, but I made it a lot when my kids were little," writes Sandra Hart of Norfolk. *"One day the little neighbor boy, Matt, was at our house and wanted a piece and asked what it was. My husband couldn't think of the name so he just called it Cherry Crab. So, since that day, that is what it has been known as."*

Mix together flour, sugar, baking powder and salt. Using electric mixer, cut butter into flour mixture. Mix egg with milk and add enough milk to make 1½ cups liquid. Batter should be thick but able to pour. Grease and flour a 15 x 10 x 1-inch pan. Pour mixture into pan. Cover with cherry pie filling. Mix flour and sugar for topping. Add butter and mix with electric mixer to make crumbly topping. Sprinkle topping over pie filling. Bake at 350° for 30-35 minutes.

Make a thin frosting with milk and powdered sugar and drizzle over cake while still warm.

CAKE
2	cups flour
1	cup sugar
2	tsp baking powder
1/2	cup butter, cut into pieces
1/4	tsp salt
1	egg
1	can cherry pie filling
	Milk

TOPPING
1	cup flour
1	cup sugar
1/2	cup butter, cut into pieces

SERVES 16-20

3/4 cup shortening
1 cup sugar
1 egg
2 tsp baking soda
1 tsp cinnamon
1 tsp ginger
1/4 cup dark molasses
2 cups flour

Makes 2-3 dozen

Marilyn's Gingersnaps
Palmer

"While helping my 95-year old aunt sort her belongings, I came across this gingersnap cookie recipe of my mother's, written by my mom and sent to my aunt," writes Marilyn Retzlaff of Palmer. "Looking for cookie recipes other than chocolate to bake for my weekly catechism students, I baked the gingersnaps and to my delight they loved the cookies. I now bake the gingersnaps often and keep the original laminated copy of my mom's recipe on my kitchen counter wall. I enjoy seeing her handwriting every day."

Mix all ingredients together. Shape into balls. Roll in sugar but don't flatten. Bake at 375° for 8 minutes.

Ice Box Cookies
Yankton, S.D.

1	cup shortening
2	beaten eggs
2	tsp baking powder
1 ½	cup sugar
3	cup flour
2/3	cup nuts
1/4	tsp salt

MAKES 2 DOZEN

"Electricity came to our farm in Madison County the fall of 1940," writes Geri Weiland Loecker of Yankton, S.D. "Although I was only four years old, I vividly remember the first purchases: an iron, washing machine and refrigerator. My mother was delighted with all three of these, but it was the refrigerator that we kids thought was magical.

"The cooled water, ice cream without cranking and ice box cookies were real treats. The cookies were special for two reasons: the nuts were black walnuts we kids harvested every year from the cow pasture, and mother baked these cookies fresh each morning for our lunch pails. Baking these cookies brings back memories of the magic of electricity and the life and love of our mother."

Cream the shortening and sugar. Add the beaten eggs, nuts, flour, salt and baking powder. Blend well. Form in a roll, wrap in waxed paper and chill overnight. Slice cookies and bake on a greased cookie sheet at 350° for 10-12 minutes.

Sour Cream Cookies
Naples, Fla.

1	cup sugar
2/3	cup butter
1	cup sour cream
4-6	cups flour
1	tsp baking soda
1	tsp salt
1	tsp baking powder

Frosting

1	box powdered sugar
1/2	cup butter, softened
1	tsp vanilla
	Milk or cream to thin as needed
6-7	drops red food coloring

MAKES 1-2 DOZEN

"My father was a Methodist minister in Meadow Grove for seven years," writes Donna Beth Linn of Naples, Fla. "My mother, Sada, loved to bake, and these cookies are favorites of all her children, grandchildren and great-grandchildren. I have no doubt they will continue on to be the favorites of the great-great-grandchildren. Mom always frosted her cookies with pink homemade frosting."

Cream butter and sugar; and add sour cream, mixing well. Combine 4 cups flour, soda, salt and baking powder (add more flour if needed). Dough should be soft but easy to handle. Refrigerate overnight. Take a small amount of dough at a time to roll out and keep the rest in the refrigerator. Roll about 1/4-inch thick. Cut with a large circle cookie cutter, or one-pound coffee can. Bake at 375° for 8-10 minutes.

To make Sada's pink frosting: In mixing bowl and using electric mixer, beat sugar, butter and vanilla. Add milk or cream as needed by spoonfuls. Add red food coloring to achieve pink color.

Frost sour cream cookies when cool. Both cookies and frosting freeze well.

1/2 cup margarine
1/2 cup shortening
1 cup white sugar
1 cup brown sugar
2 eggs
1 tsp vanilla
1 cup ground raisins
2 cups flour
1 tsp salt
1 tsp soda
2 cups ground oatmeal
1/2 cup chopped nutmeats

MAKES 6 DOZEN

FRUIT COOKIES
Kennard

"This recipe was handed down to me by my mother-in-law of German descent," writes Erma Andreasen of Kennard. "These cookies are delicious and are excellent keepers."

Cream margarine, shortening, sugars, eggs and vanilla. Stir in raisins. Stir in flour, salt and soda. Stir in ground oatmeal and nutmeats last. Drop dough by teaspoon onto cookie sheet, flatten with a glass dipped in sugar. Bake at 350° for 10 minutes or until light brown.

Hint: For easier grinding of the raisins, pour hot water over them and let stand 1 minute. Drain well before grinding.

1 ¼ cup unpopped popcorn
1/2 cup vegetable oil
1/2 cup butter or margarine
1 cup peanuts
1 6-oz bag Plain M&M's
1 lb marshmallows

SERVES 8-10

BIRTHDAY POPCORN CAKE
West Point

"This is a favorite for birthdays at our house," writes LuAnn Ortmeier of West Point.

Pop popcorn and set aside. In sauce pan, melt butter or margarine, vegetable oil and marshmallows. When butter is melted, add M&M's and peanuts. Add popcorn to sauce pan ingredients and mix thoroughly in a large mixing bowl. Butter your hands to help mix well. Press popcorn mixture into buttered angel food cake pan or Bundt pan.
Let set a few hours and remove from mold. Slice like any other cake.

POPCORN CAKE

Deshler

"This recipe was my mother-in-law's, Florence Atenhan," writes Rose Atenhan of Deshler. *"She got it from a friend back in the '70s. He gave it to her because she liked to try new things. Her doors were always open, and she always fed people a meal. I admired her stamina and energy."*

2	eggs, beaten
1 ½	cups sugar
1/4	stick melted butter
2	tsp vanilla
2	cups flour
2	tsp baking powder
1/4	tsp salt
1	cup milk
1	cup ground-up popped popcorn

Mix eggs, sugar, melted butter and vanilla. Then add flour, baking powder, salt, milk and popcorn. Mix all together and pour into a greased 9 x 13-inch pan. Bake at 350° for 1 hour.

SERVES 12

BURNT SUGAR CAKE

Grand Island

"As a young farm wife my mother, Elva McCutchan Black, was known as the 'cookie and cake lady' in the rural Grand Island area," writes Gerry Koepke of Grand Island. *"She made wonderful desserts, and my father, Roy, loved one cake in particular. He always requested her Burnt Sugar Cake for any special occasion. In Mom's handwriting on the stained and aged recipe card she notes, 'I use a little more burnt sugar syrup and a little less water. This makes a darker cake.'"*

SYRUP

1	cup granulated sugar
3/4	cup water

CAKE

1/2	cup butter
1 ½	cups granulated sugar
2	egg yolks, beaten
1	cup water
2 ½	cup flour
2	tsp baking soda
1	tsp vanilla
3	Tbsp burnt sugar syrup
2	egg whites, beaten
	Nuts if desired

FROSTING

2	cups sugar
2	Tbsp white syrup
2/3	cup water
2	Tbsp burnt sugar syrup
2	egg whites

SERVES 8-16

To make burnt sugar, cook 1 cup granulated sugar in a saucepan over high heat. Scorch sugar until very dark while stirring constantly. Add 3/4 cup water and boil until all burnt sugar is dissolved completely. This will be enough burnt sugar syrup to make several cakes. Store leftover burnt sugar syrup in an airtight container in the refrigerator.

To prepare cake cream, combine butter and 1 ½ cups sugar in large mixing bowl. Add egg yolks, beating well. Add water, flour, soda, vanilla and burnt sugar syrup. In separate bowl, beat egg whites until stiff. Fold egg whites into cake mixture. Fold nuts if desired.

Grease and flour either 2 round 8-inch cake pans or a 9 x 13-inch pan. Bake at 325° for 25 minutes, or until toothpick comes out clean.

Prepare frosting by boiling water, sugar and white syrup in medium sauce pan. Boil until it spins a thread or reaches 242° on a candy thermometer. Add burnt sugar syrup. In large mixing bowl, beat egg whites until stiff. Add hot sugar slowly to egg whites, beating until mixture is a spreadable consistency.

1   box whipped cream
1   can evaporated milk
3 ½ quarts half and half
6   beaten eggs
2 ½ cups sugar
1   2-oz bottle mapleine
    or imitation maple
    flavoring
1   cup chopped walnuts
    Dash of salt

MAKES 8 QUARTS

HOMEMADE MAPLE NUT ICE CREAM
Rochester, N.Y.

Janet McNiel Sarbou of Rochester, N.Y., sends this story and recipe:

"Growing up in Nebraska, many hours were spent cranking homemade ice cream in Grandma Glandon's old wash house in Ragan, Neb. We got a block of ice, put it into a gunny sack and beat on it with a hammer. Then we filled the bucket around the ice cream container and began to crank. Each cousin tried to crank faster than the others. When we got done we sometimes found little pieces of butter in the ice cream.

"As the recipe was handed down through the generations it has been changed, since country cream is not available today, and the amount of eggs and sugar have been lowered to make it healthier for us. Many birthdays and family reunions have been finalized with the wonderful taste of homemade maple nut ice cream."

Mix whipped cream, milk and half and half together with egg, sugar, salt, mapleine and walnuts. Put in 1 ½ gallon freezer. Prepare ice cream freezer with salt and ice as directed. Follow directions from ice cream maker for churning time.

GRANDMOTHER AEGERTER'S HOMEMADE ICE CREAM
Chadron

4-5 eggs, separated
3   cups sugar
1   Tbsp vanilla
    Dash salt
2   cups cream
3   cups milk

MAKES 2 QUARTS

"I wish my grandmothers were here to see their recipes in a cookbook!" writes Fawn Kinnamon of Chadron. "My extended families still use this recipe, and we remember having homemade ice cream socials in the summer. For the Fourth of July this year I made red and blue batches of ice cream. I also love adding coconut and other flavorings to this white ice cream. Add a malt for an even different flavor. I use an electric ice cream maker, and it is so easy."

In large mixing bowl, beat egg whites until stiff. Add 2 cups sugar slowly and beat until glossy. In separate mixing bowl, beat egg yolks until thick. Add 1 cup sugar slowly and beat until light yellow. Add yolks to whites; fold in cream, salt, vanilla and milk. Pour to fill line of ice cream freezer. Prepare ice cream freezer with ice and salt as directed. Follow directions from ice cream maker for churning time and ice cream packing when done.

PINKY THAYER

PINKY THAYER'S TIN ROOF SUNDAE
Potter

The famous Tin Roof Sundae was invented in Potter, Neb., by Pinky Thayer. Thayer's family lived above Potter Sundry where his father was the pharmacist. Pinky worked at the soda fountain and named his creation after the building's tin ceiling.

Potter Sundry and the soda fountain are still operating in the same building in downtown Potter. Here's Pinky's recipe from the Potter Historical Society:

Place one scoop of chocolate ice cream into dish and cover completely with chocolate syrup. Add one scoop of vanilla ice cream and cover generously with a layer of real marshmallow syrup until it runs off (no substitutions). Cover with peanuts and enjoy a piece of Nebraska history.

1   scoop chocolate
    ice cream
1   scoop vanilla
    ice cream
    Chocolate syrup
    Real marshmallow
    syrup
    Peanuts

MAKES 1 SUNDAE

FILLING

2 ½	cups seedless raisins
1/2	cup sugar
2	Tbsp cornstarch
3/4	cup water
3	Tbsp lemon juice

CRUMB MIXTURE

3/4	cup butter
1	cup well-packed brown sugar
1 ¾	cup flour
1/2	tsp salt
1/2	tsp baking soda
1 ½	cup rolled oats

MAKES 30 BARS

RAISIN BARS

Pierce

"This recipe is from that 1950s era and made with 'old-fashioned' ingredients like raisins, lemon and oatmeal," writes Mary Ellen Birch of Pierce. "When I was married and having my own children, I asked my mom about this recipe; I was thrilled that she still had it. I remember my grandmother fixing this for our farm lunch – and for that 4 p.m. important pick-me-up for hard-working farm hands and active children. Now my grandchildren enjoy this treat."

Cook raisins, sugar, cornstarch, water and lemon juice together until well-thickened like pie filling. Mix shortening with sugar, flour, salt and baking soda. Mix in rolled oats and flatten with hands. Place half of oat mixture into 7 x 11 x 2-inch pan. Spread raisin filling on top. Cover with remaining crumb mixture and pat down lightly. Bake at 400° for 25-30 minutes. While warm, cut into bars.

GOLD CARROT CAKE
Oklahoma City, Okla.

"This is my grandmother's recipe," writes Julie Rich, who was born and raised in McCook and now lives in Oklahoma City. "She was a farmer's wife and in my opinion she was the best cook ever! What I loved about eating at her home was that everything was homemade. Most of the time she didn't even cook with a recipe. This is one of my favorite desserts she baked."

Set out butter and cream cheese to soften at room temperature. Grease a 9 x 13-inch pan or two 8-inch pans, or line with greased waxed paper for easy clean up and cake removal.

Combine flour, baking powder, soda, salt and cinnamon. Beat eggs; add sugar and oil. Mix well. Blend in carrots and drained pineapple. Stir in dry ingredients. Add nuts and coconut. Bake at 350° for 25-30 minutes. The 9 x 13-inch pan will take longer to cook.

To make the frosting, in a separate small bowl, cream together 1/2 cup softened butter or margarine and 1 package softened cream cheese. Add 1 tsp vanilla and beat in 1 lb confectioner's sugar. Frost cake after it has cooled.

CAKE
2	cups flour, sifted
2	tsp baking powder
1 ½	tsp baking soda
1	tsp salt
2	tsp cinnamon
2	cups sugar
1 ½	cups salad oil
4	eggs
2	cups carrots, finely grated
1	8-oz can crushed pineapple, drained
1/2	cups nuts, chopped
1	cup coconut

FROSTING
1/2	cup butter or margarine, softened
1	8-oz package cream cheese, softened
1	lb confectioner's sugar
1	tsp vanilla

SERVES 10-12

APPLE CAKE
Omaha

Babe McDaniel of Omaha sends this recipe, a favorite of her morning walking friends. "After our walks we all sit down and enjoy this wonderfully moist cake with coffee."

Combine egg, 1 cup sugar, margarine and hot coffee. Sift together in a separate bowl, flour, baking soda, 1/2 tsp cinnamon and cloves. Mix all together and add apples and walnuts. Pour into a greased 8 x 8-inch pan and top with remaining cinnamon and sugar. Bake at 350° for 25 minutes. Cut into squares when cooled and serve with whipped cream.

1	beaten egg
1 ¼	cup sugar
1/2	cup margarine, unmelted
1/2	cup hot coffee
1	tsp baking soda
1 ½	cups flour
1 ½	tsp cinnamon
1/4	tsp ground cloves
1	cup chopped and peeled tart apple
	Walnuts (as desired)

SERVES 8

8   quarts popped
     corn (old maids
     removed)
1   cup butter or
     margarine
1/2 cup white corn syrup
9   oz Red Hot candy*

MAKES 8 QUARTS

BIG RED (HOT) POPCORN
Creighton

"As I do most of my 'tailgating' from home, this is easy to carry anywhere," writes
*Beverly Schwindt of Creighton. "This is a crunchy popcorn snack that has a flavor like
no other and matches our unique Big Red team."*

Spray a large baking sheet with vegetable spray. In a medium sauce pan, combine
butter, syrup and Red Hot candy. Stir until the candy is melted. Place popcorn on
baking sheet; pour candy over the popcorn and bake at 250° for 1 hour, stirring
every 15 minutes. Let cool and enjoy the unique flavor.

*If Red Hot brand candy is not available, substitute cinnamon imperials or Hot
Tamales candy as we did for the photo.

O'HENRY BARS

Stapleton

6	cups old fashioned oatmeal
1	cup melted margarine
1 ½	cups firmly packed brown sugar
4 ½	tsp vanilla
3/4	cup white corn syrup
3/4	cup chunky peanut butter
1	12-oz package chocolate baking chips

MAKES 24-36 BARS

"I made this recipe often when my children were young because it made a lot of bars and also because it was such a healthy mixture for them to snack on and use for dessert," writes Carol Burgess of Stapleton. "This was also a favorite with the adult crowd. I served it often for my ladies bridge clubs."

Mix and spread everything but peanut butter and baking chips in two greased 15 x 13-inch jelly roll pans. The mixture will be stiff; use vegetable or butter spray on utensil to spread. Bake at 350° for 12 minutes. While oatmeal crust is baking, melt together peanut butter mixture and baking chips. When crust is almost cool, spread the chocolate mixture over the tops. Cool completely and cut into bars.

OVEN CARAMEL POPCORN

O'Neill

1	large pan of popped corn, or 4 bags or microwave popcorn
2	cups brown sugar
1	cup butter or margarine
1/2	cup white corn syrup
1	tsp salt
1	tsp baking soda
1	tsp vanilla or butter flavoring
	Nuts if desired

MAKES 12-16 CUPS

"I had two boys who wrestled, and gaining weight over the holidays was a 'no-no,' "writes MaryAnn Nissen of O'Neill. "Instead of making candy or baked goods, I made caramel popcorn so they could have a treat without the extra calories. This was back in the 1970s, but I continue to make the caramel popcorn for Christmas and give them their own bags. Then they don't steal from the grandkids!"

Pop enough popcorn to fill a roaster or large baking pan. In medium saucepan, combine brown sugar, butter, syrup and salt. Bring to a boil and cook for 5 minutes, stirring well. Remove from heat; add soda and flavorings. Stir until frothy. Pour over popped corn; add nuts if desired. Mix well.

Place in oven at 250° for 1 hour, stirring every 15 minutes. Spread on cookie sheets or newspapers to cool. Store in covered containers to keep crisp.

3 eggs
1 tsp salt
1 ½ cups sugar
2 cup flour
2 tsp baking powder
1 cup cold water
1 tsp vanilla
1 cup powdered sugar
1 Tbsp milk
Chopped peanuts
or shredded coconut
for topping

Serves 12

Joann's Cake
Ogallala

"This recipe came from our mother, who died a few days before her 104th birthday. She grew up in the Cairo area of Nebraska and her family spoke German prior to World War I," writes Joann Daubendiek of Ogallala. "The origin of this recipe is unknown, but it was made at Christmas time."

Beat eggs and salt for 2 minutes. Add sugar and beat 5 minutes. Add 1 cup flour, sifted with baking powder and beat 2 minutes. Add 1 cup flour, cold water and vanilla and beat well. Pour into greased 9 x 13-inch pan. Bake at 350° for 25-30 minutes or until toothpick comes out clean. Mix milk and powdered sugar to create icing. When cool, cut cake into squares, spread sides with icing (hold two sides with fingers and don't ice those sides). Roll in peanuts or coconut.

Connie's Kickin' Key Lime Pie
Norfolk

5 egg yolks, beaten
1 14-oz can sweetened condensed milk
1 9-inch prepared graham cracker crust
1/2 cup key lime juice
1 7-oz jar marshmallow creme
Whipped topping
Lime slices

Serves 8

Nebraska re-comer, Connie Oringderff, dropped off this key lime pie, story and original recipe to our magazine office. She had a quest while living in Florida to find – and make – the perfect key lime pie. Now, she's brought it back to Nebraska.

"This is a very easy key lime pie recipe," she said. "When I lived in Florida, almost every place advertised the 'best key lime pie.' My husband and I traveled around and would always order key lime pie. I started playing around with different recipes and think I created the best key lime pie. Most key lime pies have egg base and sweetened condensed milk. My special recipe was adding marshmallow creme. I've never seen it in any recipe books."

Preheat oven to 375°. Combine egg yolks, sweetened condensed milk, lime juice and marshmallow creme. Mix well. Pour into unbaked graham cracker shell. Bake for 20 minutes. Cool. Garnish with whipped topping and lime slices twisted into an "s" shape.

Pumpkin Pie
McCook

1 large can pumpkin
7 large beaten eggs
3 tsp cinnamon
3 tsp ginger
1 tsp salt
3 cups of half and half
4 prepared pie crusts

Makes 4 pies

Jenny Colby of McCook sends the following note and pumpkin pie recipe:

"My Grandmother was born in 1900 and had lots of great recipes. My mother and I discovered that most of her recipes were never written down as we were planning a family cookbook for everyone. The task was much harder than we thought because so many were from memory."

Combine sugar and spices. Turn pumpkin into bowl adding the rest of the ingredients gradually. Pour evenly into pie shells and bake at 450° for 12 minutes. Turn oven down to 350° for another hour or until knife inserted comes out clean.

FIRST LAYER
1   cup butter
2   Tbsp sugar
2   cups flour
1/2 tsp salt

SECOND LAYER
5   cups diced rhubarb
4   Tbsp flour
2   cup sugar
1/4 tsp salt
6   egg yolks
1   cup cream

THIRD LAYER
6   egg whites
3/4 cup sugar
2   tsp vanilla
     Dash of salt

SERVES 12

MOM'S EASIER RHUBARB TORTE
Yankton, S.D.

"My mom Helen Zimmerman, now 92, lives in Lincoln and raised a large family cooking for seven children and a husband," writes Lois Varvel of Yankton, S.D. "My father was a minister, and with his relocations to other parishes we lived in five states. We ended up in Creston in the 1960s as our first Nebraska residence. My mom came across this recipe in the 1970s, and after years of making it found a way to simplify it as a one-step/one-pan recipe. She says her mouth waters every time she speaks of her rhubarb torte."

Crumble together first-layer ingredients. Generously grease a 9 x 13-inch pan. Pat crust in pan. Bake at 350° for 10 minutes. The crust should be dry, but not brown.

Mix together second-layer ingredients. Pour over crust and bake at 375° for 40-45 minutes, or until firm.

Beat egg whites for the third layer until stiff. Add sugar, 2 Tbsp at a time, thoroughly mixing in all sugar. Add vanilla and salt; mix well. Pour over custard filling. If desired, sprinkle with nuts or coconut. Bake at 350° for 10-15 minutes, just to brown meringue tips

OATMEAL CAKE

Ord

"This is a favorite to take to potlucks," writes Gladys Nolte of Ord. "I take it to church when they ask for a dessert. The pan always comes home empty. This recipe was given to me many years ago by a good friend."

In medium mixing bowl, combine boiling water, oatmeal, butter and salt. Let stand 20 minutes. In large mixing bowl, cream sugars with eggs. Add flour, soda and cinnamon. Add oatmeal mixture and mix cake by hand, using a wooden spoon, as it is too thick for a mixer. Beat well. Pour cake mixture into a greased and flour a 9 x 13-inch pan. Bake at 350° for 25-30 minutes or until toothpick comes out clean.

Prepare frosting by mixing butter, brown sugar, milk, vanilla and coconut or walnuts together in a small mixing bowl. Frost immediately after removing cake from the oven. Broil cake and frosting for 2 minutes. Cool and serve.

CAKE

1 ¼	cup boiling water
1	cup quick oatmeal
1/2	cup butter or margarine
1/2	tsp salt
1	cup granulated sugar
1	cup brown sugar
2	eggs
1 ⅓	cup flour
1	tsp baking soda
1	tsp cinnamon

FROSTING

6	Tbsp melted butter or margarine
2/3	cup brown sugar
1/4	cup evaporated milk or heavy cream
1	tsp vanilla
1/2	cup coconut or walnuts

SERVES 12-16

GRANDMA GRACE'S BUTTERSCOTCH PIE

Randolph

"This is a favorite recipe I learned to make 50-some years ago when I was a new bride from my mother-in-law Grace Huwaldt, who was a super pie baker," writes Virginia Huwaldt. "I will say, many years later, I mastered the recipe well enough to get a few compliments."

Mix together brown sugar and butter. Add evaporated milk to moisten well. Boil this a short time and set aside to cool. When cool, add flour, water, milk, egg yolks and salt. Return to heat and stir until thick; add vanilla and pour into 9-inch baked crust. Use egg whites for meringue.

1 ¼	cup brown sugar
2	Tbsp butter
1/4	cup evaporated milk
3	Tbsp flour
1	cup water
2	egg yolks
1/4	tsp salt
1	tsp vanilla
1	cup milk

SERVES 8

CAKE

3 ½ cups flour
3 tsp baking powder
1 cup sugar
3/4 tsp salt
2 eggs, beaten
1 ½ cup milk
3/4 cup melted butter
or shortening

TOPPING

1/2 cup sugar
1/2 cup margarine
or butter
1/3 cup flour
1 ½ Tbsp cinnamon
1/2 tsp salt

SERVES 24

BROWNIES

4 squares chocolate
1 cup butter or
margarine
4 eggs
2 cups sugar
2 cups flour
1 tsp vanilla
1 cup chopped nuts
1 7-oz jar marshmal-
low creme
Pinch of salt

FROSTING

1 cup sugar
5 Tbsp butter or
margarine
1/3 cup milk
1 16-oz package
semi-sweet
chocolate chips

MAKES 16 BROWNIES

DAD'S COFFEECAKE

Osmond

"My dad made this coffee cake every Sunday when he worked as a baker at Wayne State College in the 1970s," writes Joyce Tacey of Osmond. "It has become a family favorite. His granddaughter has received several purple ribbons at the fair with this recipe and we also make it for every special occasion."

Mix together flour, baking powder, sugar and salt. Add eggs and milk, then shortening. Spread half of dough in bottom of a 9 x 13 x 2-inch pan. Combine topping ingredients and sprinkle half of it over dough in pan. Add remainder of dough, then remainder of topping. Bake at 375° for 25-30 minutes.

LAVON'S BROWNIES

Grand Island

"These brownies are my family's favorite," writes LaVon Mason of Grand Island. "They are rich, but good!"

In small saucepan, melt butter and chocolate squares. Remove from heat and set aside. In large mixing bowl, beat eggs and sugar until smooth. Mix in melted chocolate and butter. Add flour, salt, vanilla and nuts, mixing well. Pour into a 15 x 10-inch jelly-roll pan. Bake at 350° for 15-20 minutes. Spread marshmallow creme over brownies while warm.

In a small pan, combine sugar, butter and milk. Broil one minute, stirring constantly; remove from heat. Stir in chocolate chips until smooth. Pour or spread over marshmallow creme immediately.

Cola Cake

Madison

"This recipe has evolved to this place after many experiments," writes Carol Robertson of Madison. *"Between teaching home economics and helping with 4-H, the kids came up with a fun liquid substitute for a cake recipe, and the 'Cola-Cake' was born. It made learning fun. I increased ingredients to make this a sheet cake, and it's kind of a cross between a cake and a brownie. I have even made cupcakes and used the frosting as a filling."*

Combine flour and sugar very thoroughly in mixing bowl. Combine margarine, oil, cocoa and cola in saucepan or microwave and bring to a boil. Remove from heat immediately. Beat hot mixture into flour-sugar mixture. In a separate small bowl, mix buttermilk with soda, eggs and flavorings. Blend all together with a mixer. Place in greased and floured or wax-paper-lined pan and bake at 350° for 35 minutes. Leave cake in pan and let cool.

For frosting, bring margarine, cocoa and cola to a boil. Beat together flavorings and enough powdered sugar to make a frosting that will pour from the pan and yet hold its shape on the cake.

CAKE

3	cups all purpose flour
3	cups granulated sugar
3/4	cup salad oil
3/4	cup margarine
1/4	cup cocoa
1 ½	cola
3/4	cup buttermilk
1 ½	tsp baking soda
3	eggs
1 ½	tsp butter flavoring
1 ½	tsp burnt sugar flavoring

FROSTING

1/2	cup margarine
3	Tbsp cocoa
6	Tbsp cola soft drink
1	tsp butter flavoring
1	tsp burnt sugar flavoring
	Powdered sugar

SERVES 12

1   15-oz can apricots,
    drained
1   cup unsweetened
    apple sauce
1/2 cup cornstarch
1/2 cup water
2/3 cup sugar
1   egg yolk
1   Tbsp butter
1   Tbsp vanilla
1   precooked pie crust

SERVES 8

APRICOT-APPLE PIE
Gordon

"I love to cook and bake," writes Laveta Cole of Gordon. "I am always making up new recipes. This is one of my most recent experiments combining apples and apricots, because you don't usually see that. My daughter asked me to write this down for her as it has become one of our most recent favorites. Be sure you have enough cornstarch to make the applesauce hold firm, as it tends to get runny. I have tried meringue and whipped topping, and we prefer the whipped topping."

In a medium saucepan, mix apricot halves and applesauce together. Cook on medium heat until just bubbly. In measuring cup, combine water, cornstarch and sugar. Add to fruit and stir constantly until cornstarch becomes clear and fruit is thickened. Turn off heat. Add egg yolk, butter and vanilla. Stir until all ingredients are blended. Pour into baked pie crust. Chill at least 1 hour. Top with whipped topping or meringue.

Mrs. Donahue's Applesauce Cake

Colts Neck, N.J.

"This recipe was given to my mom by Mrs. Donahue while we lived in Harrison," writes Ellen Krupa of Colts Neck, N.J. *"My sisters and I still use this recipe. It is wonderful, moist and keeps very well when wrapped tightly in the refrigerator. Mrs. Donahue was a dear Irish lady. Her recipe lives on."*

Beat sugar and butter until creamy. Add applesauce and soda. Add flour and spices, raisins and nuts. Pour into large greased and floured loaf pan, and bake at 350° for 50-60 minutes or until toothpick comes clean.

1	cup sugar
1/2	cup butter
2	cups flour
1 ½	cups unsweetened applesauce
2	tsp soda dissolved in 1 Tbsp hot water
1	tsp cloves
1	tsp cinnamon
1	cup raisins
1	cup chopped nuts

MAKES 1 LARGE LOAF

Penuche Frosting

Omaha

"This was my mother's favorite frosting for spice cake and can be used on banana cookies as well," writes Adriane Mazuch of Omaha. *"It is so easy to make and the brown sugar gives it unbeatable flavor."*

Melt butter in medium sauce pan. Add brown sugar and cook on medium heat for 2 minutes. Add milk and bring to a boil. Remove pan from heat and cool. And add vanilla and enough powdered sugar to thicken as you like.

1/2	cup butter
1	cup brown sugar
1/4	cup milk
1	tsp vanilla Confectioner's sugar (powdered sugar)

MAKES 2 CUPS FROSTING

GRAPE PIE
Scottsbluff

3 cups fresh
    Concord grapes
1/2-1 cup sugar
3 Tbsp flour
1 Tbsp lemon juice
1 Tbsp butter, melted
    Double crust pastry
    for 9-inch pie

SERVES 8

*"My grandmother Florence Firme Gueck moved to Scottsbluff by wagon in 1914,"
writes Joan Koehler of Scottsbluff. "Her family thought she was moving to the 'ends of
the earth, way out west.'*

*"Grandma was a wonderful cook. She made her own cookbook that was a
handwritten collection of her tried-and-true recipes, kept in an olive green loose-leaf
notebook. She also kept in the notebook clippings of helpful hints and recipes from
friends. I still have it and hope to pass it on to my son one day. The grape pie is one of
her unusual favorites."*

Wash and stem the grapes. Remove skins by squeezing grapes gently. Reserve the
skins and place pulp in a large saucepan. Heat pulp to boiling, stirring occasionally.
Reduce heat and simmer 5 minutes, or until the seeds can easily be removed by
pressing pulp through a sieve. Discard seeds and mix pulp with skins, sugar, flour,
lemon juice and butter.

Pour into an unbaked pie shell and make a lattice crust for top. Sprinkle top with
sugar. Bake at 425° for 10 minutes, then reduce heat to 350° for 30 minutes.

Today, you can get seedless Concord grapes and avoid the sieve to remove the
seeds. Simmer the grapes for 5 minutes and the skins will come off. Then add the
remaining ingredients as above.

*Our Nebraska Kitchens staff used red table grapes for this recipe as Concord grapes
were not available. We also did not remove the skins, but cooked the grapes whole. It
was delicious.*

1 cup nut meats,
  chopped
1 cup chopped dates
1 cup powdered sugar
2 eggs, save white of
  1 egg, beaten
1 unbaked pie crust

SERVES 6-8

CHICAGO PIE
Ericson

"This is one my mother always baked at Christmas time," writes Bonnadel Foster of Ericson. "This was back in the 1930s when money was not plentiful but she always had Chicago pie for our Christmas dinner. We had our own whipping cream as we milked cows at that time."

Mix together nuts, dates, powdered sugar and eggs. Add beaten egg white and a little milk to moisten. Pour into pie crust and bake at 350° for 30 minutes. Serve with whipped cream.

1 ½ cups sugar
3/4 cup butter
1 5-oz can
evaporated milk
2 4.67-oz packages
mint, cherry or
toffee Andes
Candies (56
pieces total)
1 7-oz jar marshmal-
low creme
22 oz white baking
chocolate
1/2 cup semisweet
chocolate chips
Food coloring,
optional

MAKES 8 DOZEN

HEARTY TRUE LOVE TRUFFLES

Ainsworth

"I tasted these at a quilt show a few years ago and got the recipe and entered it in 'The Middle of Nowhere…Chocolate Fair' in Ainsworth," writes Ione Bruveleit. "I even won a prize for them! I am not a mint fan, so I only use the toffee and cherry flavored Andes candy. Almond bark is not as soft as chocolate chips for dipping, so I combine the two. I usually make these for the holidays."

In heavy saucepan, combine sugar, butter and milk. Bring to a boil over medium heat, stirring constantly. Reduce heat; cook and stir until a candy thermometer reads 236° (soft ball stage). Remove from heat.

Stir in candies until melted and mixture is well blended. Stir in marshmallow creme and vanilla until smooth. Spread into a buttered 15 x 10 inch x 1-inch pan; cover and refrigerate for 1 hour.

Cut into 96 pieces; roll each into a ball. Place on a waxed paper-lined baking sheet. Freeze for one hour.

In heavy saucepan or microwave-safe bowl, melt 18 oz of white chocolate and chocolate chips together. Dip frozen balls into melted chocolate. Place on waxed paper to harden.

Melt the remaining white chocolate, add food coloring if desired. Drizzle over truffles. Store in an airtight container in the refrigerator.

PINK PEPPERMINT ICE

Hastings

10	oz white candy coating
2	Tbsp crushed peppermint candies, about 7
1/4	tsp peppermint extract
2	drops red food coloring

MAKES 10 OUNCES

"My granddaughter Sarina, age 8, likes to make food in the microwave," writes Ruth Janssen of Hastings. "This one is one of her favorites, especially at Christmas time."

Crush peppermint candies and set aside. Lay out a sheet of waxed paper. In a microwave bowl melt candy coating, heating 30 seconds at a time, stirring after each 30 seconds; cook until smooth. Remove bowl from microwave and add crushed candies, flavoring and food coloring. Spread on waxed paper to cool completely. Break into small pieces. Store in an airtight container.

LIME DESSERT

Pender

"This dessert was a Christmas tradition in our hometown of Lyons," writes Dee Roeber of Pender. "My mother was a very good cook, and she let my sister and me watch her do her magic in that kitchen. I am very thankful for the love of cooking she gave me, and I am passing that on to my sons who are now very good cooks."

1	3-oz package lime Jell-O
1/4	tsp green food coloring
1	cup sugar
1/4	cup lemon juice
1	can evaporated milk
2	cups Oreo cookies, crushed
1/3	cup melted butter
1½	cups English walnuts, chopped
1 ¾	cup boiling water Shaved sweet chocolate

SERVES 9-12

In medium mixing bowl, combine Jell-O, boiling water, food coloring, sugar, lemon and lemon juice. Chill in refrigerator for several hours or until almost set, then with electric mixer whip Jell-O and transfer to a large bowl. In separate medium bowl, whip evaporated milk until thick. Fold whipped milk into Jell-O. In a 9 x 13-inch pan, combine crushed cookies and melted butter. Press into pan. Pour Jell-O mixture over cookie crumb crust. Use vegetable peeler to create chocolate shavings. Sprinkle chocolate shavings and walnuts over Jell-O. Chill several hours before serving.

L ET US SHOW YOU
AN INFORMAL ARRANGEMENT
that can work for holidays and special
occasions. Save the formal dinner settings and all
their measurements and requirements for the cruise
or wedding. You can set a lovely table using proper
informal table etiquette. Our few guidelines listed here
will make you the "hostess-with-the-mostess" to your
guests and family. Everyone will think they have come
to a five-star dining experience.

So relax, mix and match grandma's plates, Aunt June's
linens, and go ahead and use the good silver. It's your
party.

A few hard and fast rules include forks on the left,
knives and spoons on the right. How many forks and
spoons? Generally, it depends on how many courses.
Every course should have its own set of utensils. Every
course should have its own beverage, and water should
be available at all times. Napkins can go on the plate,
beside the forks or under the forks depending on the
space provided.

Our photo shows a four-course table setting of soup
and bread, salad, main course and dessert. The dessert
utensils are always at the top of the dinner plate. The
beverage combinations are water, and wine for all
courses, with coffee and champagne saved for dessert.
There are no rules but your rules with the beverages.
Serve what your guests will enjoy. Informally you can
share the salt and pepper, cream and sugar and food can
be served from the table. Enjoy!

**Entertain family and friends with a "fancy" table setting, modified
from formal rules for our casual Nebraska lifestyle.**

Fancy Tabl

Bread Knife

Bread Plate

Dinner Fork

Salad Fork

Napkin

Setting for Nebraskans

Champagne Glass

Wine Glass

Water Glass

Coffee Cup

Coffee Teaspoon

Dessert Fork

Dessert Spoon

Coffee Saucer

Dessert Plate

Soup Bowl

Soup Spoon

Salad Plate

Dinner Plate

Steak Knife

Dinner Knife

Dinner Teaspoon

Tips from the Kitchen

When perusing and using old recipes, these conversions, substitutions and tips will help you along the way:

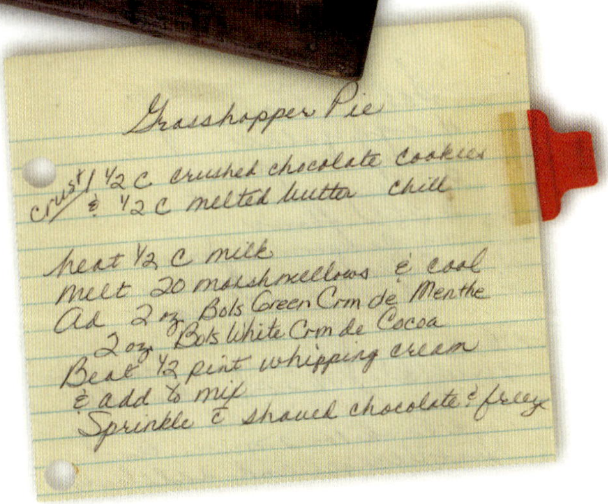

CONVERSIONS

#1 tall can =	**2 cups**
#2 can =	**2 ½ cups**
#2 ½ can =	**3 ½ cups**
#3 can =	**4 ¼ cups**
#10 can =	**13 cups**
#303 can =	**2 cups**
Dash =	**10 drops**
A few grains =	**1/8 tsp**
6 dashes =	**1 tsp**
5 milliliters =	**1 tsp**
28 grams =	**1 oz**
Jigger =	**1 ½ oz**
Oleo =	**Margarine**
Handful =	**1/2 cup**
Scant =	**Less than a full measure, not level**
Heaping =	**Over the full measure, above level**
Pinch =	**1/8-1/4 tsp**
1 lb =	**2 cups butter**
	4 cups flour
	2 cups sugar
	3 ½ cups powdered sugar
	2 ⅔ cups brown sugar
	2 cups milk

Grasshopper Pie

Crust 1 ½ C crushed chocolate cookies
& ½ C melted butter   chill

heat ½ C milk
Melt 20 marshmallows & cool
Add 2 oz Bols Green Crm de Menthe
2 oz Bols White Crm de Cocoa
Beat ½ pint whipping cream
& add to mix
Sprinkle & shaved chocolate & freely

SUBSTITUTIONS

Allspice
Amount: 1 tsp
Substitute: 1/2 tsp cinnamon plus 1/2 tsp ground cloves

Apple pie spice
Amount: 1 tsp
Substitute: 1/2 tsp cinnamon plus 1/4 tsp nutmeg, plus 1/8 tsp cardamom

Baking powder, double-acting
Amount: 1 tsp
Substitute: 1/4 tsp baking soda plus 5/8 tsp cream of tarter

Beer
Substitute: Nonalcoholic beer, apple cider or beef broth

Butter
Amount: 1 cup
Substitute: 1/2 cup margarine plus 1/2 cup vegetable shortening (Crisco)

Buttermilk
Amount: 1 cup
Substitute: 1 Tbsp lemon juice or vinegar plus enough regular milk to make 1 cup. Allow to stand 5 minutes. Or use 1 cup plain yogurt.

Chocolate, unsweetened
Amount: 1 oz
Substitute: 3 Tbsp cocoa plus 1 Tbsp butter, margarine or vegetable oil

Cornstarch for thickening
Amount: 1 Tbsp
Substitute: 2 Tbsp flour. Cook 3 minutes after thickened to avoid raw taste of flour. Or use 4 tsp quick-cooking tapioca.

Flour, all-purpose white flour
Amount: 1 cup
Substitute: 1/2 cup whole wheat flour plus 1/2 cup all-purpose flour. Substituting more than half of the all-purpose flour with wheat flour will reduce volume and result in heavier product.

Flour, self-rising
Amount: 1 cup
Substitute: 1 cup minus 2 Tbsp all-purpose flour plus 1 1/2 tsp baking powder and 1/2 tsp salt

Flour, cake
Amount: 1 cup
Substitute: 1 cup minus 2 Tbsp all-purpose flour

Marshmallows, miniature
Amount: 1 cup
Substitute: 10 large marshmallows

Mayonnaise, for use in salads and salad dressings
Amount: 1 cup
Substitute: 1 cup sour cream, 1 cup yogurt or 1 cup cottage cheese pureed in blender

Sugar, confectioners' or powdered
Amount: 1 cup
Substitute: 1 cup granulated sugar plus 1 Tbsp cornstarch. Blend with metal blade in food processor or powdery.

Wine, red
Substitute: Same amount of grape or cranberry juice

Wine, white
Substitute: Same amount of apple or white grape juice

Yeast, compressed
Amount: 1 cake (3/5 oz)
Substitute: 1 package (1/4 oz) active dry yeast or scant 2 ½ tsp loose active dry yeast

Index

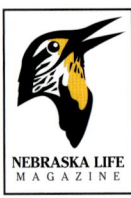

NEBRASKA LIFE

Nebraska Life Publishing, Inc.

Publisher/President:
Christopher Amundson
Vice President: Angela Amundson

**Nebraska Kitchens Cookbook Volume 2:
Favorite Recipes of Our State
Compiled by *Nebraska Life Magazine***

Recipes and Stories Coordinators:
Noreen Crawford and Angela Amundson
Chief Editor/Photographer:
Christopher Amundson
Design Team: Camille Kirchhoff and
Anthony Kuhlmann

Contributing Writers:
Whitney Keyes
Kristen Friesen

**The following people provided
additional photography:**
Bobbi and Steve Olson
Tuscan Villa Bed & Breakfast, pp. 42-43
High Plains Homestead's
Drifter Cookshack, pp. 64-65
Henderson Mennonites, pp. 82-85
Darin Epperly
Mom's Marinated Carrots, p. 68
Chocolate Cake Roll, p. 92
Lydia Christian
The Feed Barn Restaurant, p. 4

Manufactured in U.S.A.

Back cover photos (clockwise
from top left): Indian Taco;
Pork Roast with Parsnips;
Corn and Tomato Salad; Mom's
Easier Rhubarb Torte; Triple
Berry Zucchini Bread.

Send us your favorite family recipes!

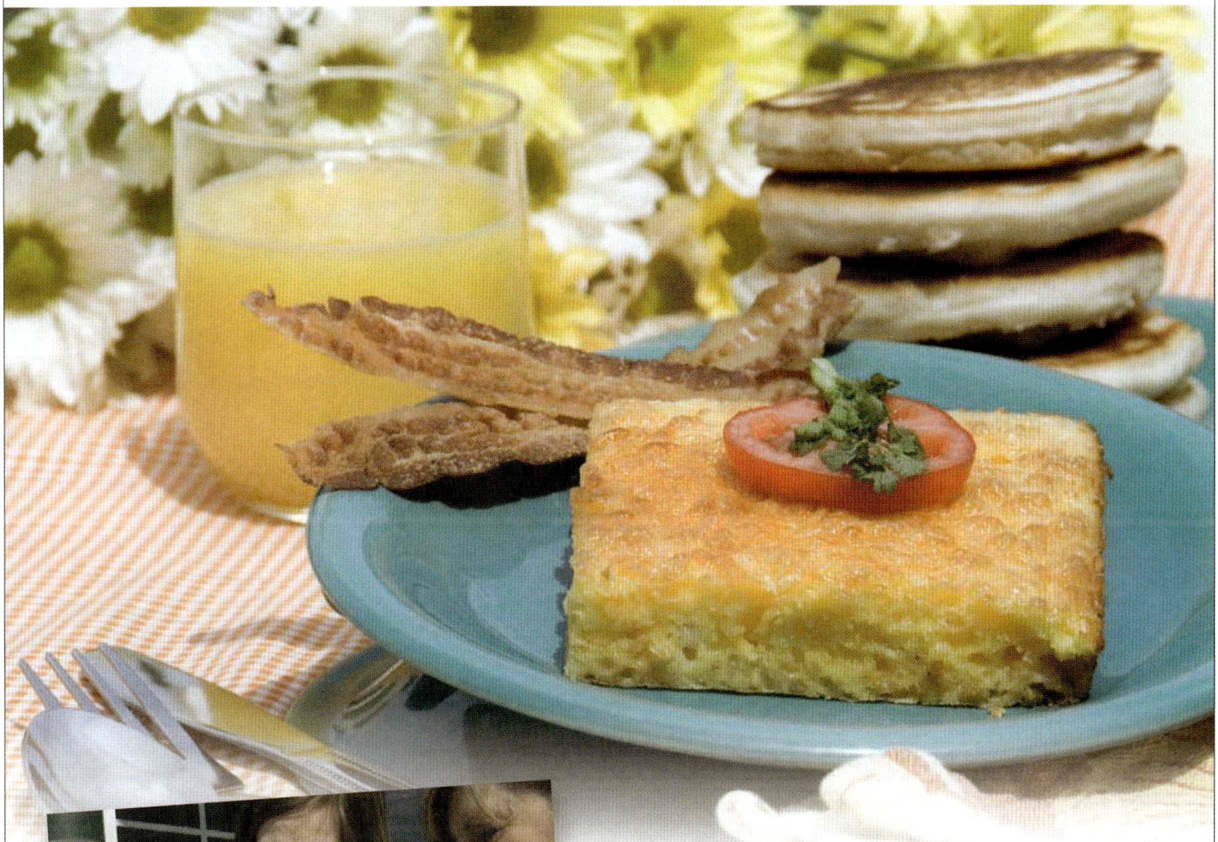

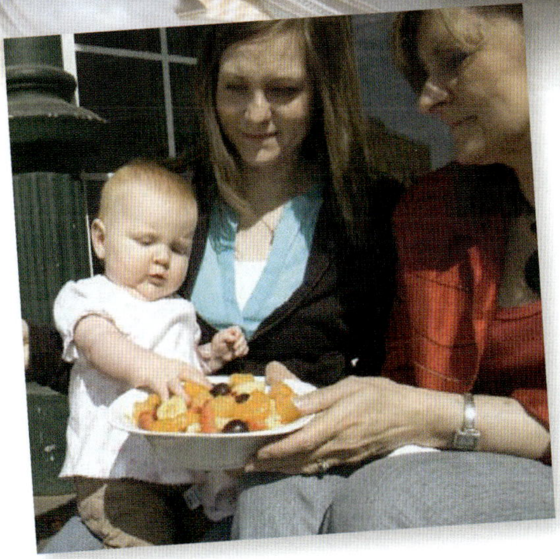

Nebraska Life Magazine is always looking for favorite family recipes from Nebraskans and former Nebraskans. We're especially interested in recipes that have been passed down from one generation to the next and the stories that go along with them.

You can send your recipes to:

Nebraska Kitchens
c/o Nebraska Life Magazine
PO Box 819, Norfolk, NE 68702-0819
kitchens@nebraskalife.com

NEBRASKA LIFE

The Magazine That Explores Nebraska

206 Norfolk Avenue • 800-777-6159 • www.NebraskaLife.com

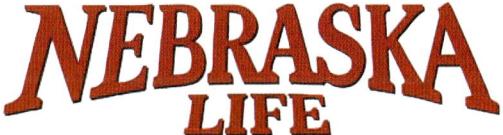

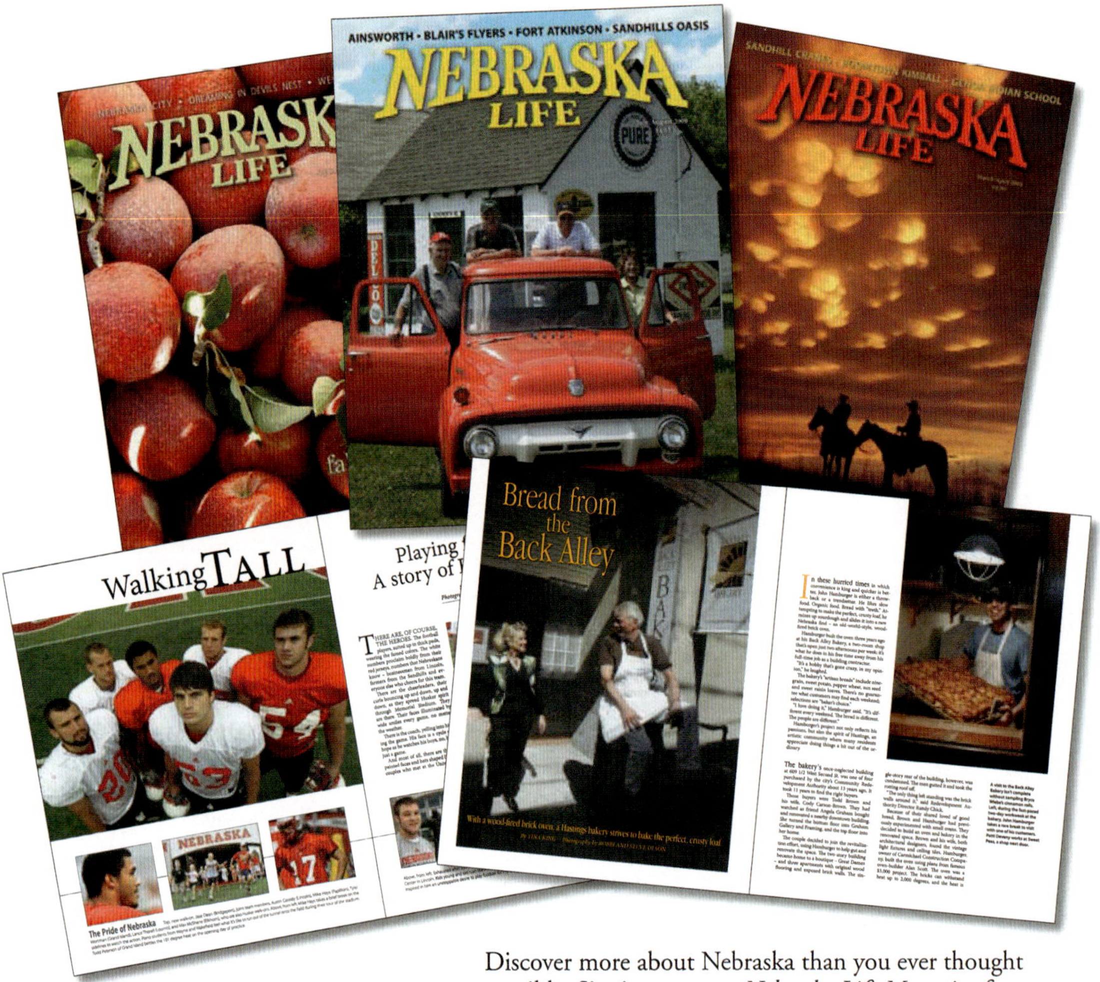